MARKER KAI

UNDERSTANDING LINUX
INTERNALS
AND TROUBLESHOOTING

THE
LINUX
— SYSTEMS —
INTERVIEW

Table of Contents

Preface **6**

Introduction **9**

Chapter 1: Interrupts **11**

How Interrupts Work.. 11

Questions..16

Chapter 2: System Calls **17**

Access Rings 17

System Calls 19

How System Calls Work.......................................19

Common System Calls 22

Linux Commands to Inspect System Calls 27

Questions.. 29

Chapter 3: Processes **31**

Overview..31

Internal Structure 32

Process Memory Layout...................................... 34

Process Lifecycle 35

Zombie & Orphan Process 37

Questions.. 39

Chapter 4: Memory Management **40**

Memory Management Unit (MMU) 41

Questions.. 44

Chapter 5: Memory Allocation **45**

Using the Heap 46

Using the Stack 48

Questions 50

Chapter 6: Signals **51**

Common Signals...52

Fatal Signals..53

Signals in Action: nohup 54

Procfs 55

Questions 58

Chapter 7: Scheduling **59**

Linux Scheduler...59

Process States 61

Signals and States...62

Changing Priority 63

Questions 65

Chapter 8: Linux I/O Model.................... **66**

Overview 66

Advantages...67

Systems Calls 68

File Descriptors 69

How Processes Use File Descriptors 71

System Call Examples......................................72

Pipes...76

Questions 79

Chapter 9: Linux File System Implementation........ 80

Overview..80

Ext2 81

Ext2 Data Blocks 82

Inode Table... 83

Directories and File Resolution 84

Hard and Soft Links 85

Inode Table in Action... 87

Questions...90

Chapter 10: Sockets 91

Overview...91

System Calls 93

Unix Domain Sockets.. 94

Questions... 95

Chapter 11: Boot Process 96

Overview.. 96

Questions... 98

Chapter 12: Troubleshooting 99

Fundamental Analysis 99

Common Tools 100

Scenarios 120

Answers to Questions 125

Preface

This book is intended to prepare you for the Linux systems interview at big tech FAANG-typed companies. These companies have particular job roles with dedicated Linux systems interviews that go deep into Linux internals. The roles go by different names at different companies (SRE, Production Engineer, Systems Development Engineer, etc.), but the skill set required for all of them are more-or-less the same: coding, system design, Linux, and networking. There are many great interview books on the preparation for coding and system design interviews but none specifically for networking and Linux interviews. The networking interview tends to go less deep than the others and rather assesses broadly across fundamental networking concepts (e.g., DNS, HTTP, SSL, TCP, UDP). For specific networking roles, there may dive deeper into networking, e.g. routing protocols. The Linux systems interview, however, often goes very deep. The interviewer will generally push you as far as you can go on any of the Linux internals topics.

This book will aid you in preparing for the Linux systems interview. For many engineers, even if they are daily Linux users, there's a high chance that they're not familiar with the internals of the Linux operating system. For example, most users know how to list the files in a directory with ls and check more information on each file using ls -l, and maybe even know how to check if they're linked to another file or directory on the file system. But not all users know how the kernel locates the directory inode, lists the files in the directory's data blocks, finds each file inode, and gets its metadata from the inode table to return to the ls -l cmd. Similarly, many users know how to write a script into a file, make it executable, run it, and pipe its output to another command like grep. However, not all users know that to make all of that happen, a software interrupt is triggered, values are loaded into kernel registers, a range of system calls are invoked to create processes, perform IPC, file descriptors are opened and closed, etc.

Now, it's not unreasonable to question the relevance of some of these internal mechanics to the job being applied for. Similar arguments can and have been made for some convoluted DS&A coding questions that most developers will never use in their job. This book will not attempt to answer these types of questions. We'll just say that these FAANG companies have a high bar, and they try to ensure that the engineers hired for these roles are equipped with the knowledge and skills needed to approach and solve any technical challenge they may come across in their problem space.

If you look through the table of contents and are already familiar with each of the topics covered, then you're probably ready to take the interview. If you're not sure, then this book can help you prepare. If you're absolutely new to Linux and have a Linux interview lined up for one of these roles, this book should not be your first step in preparing. You should first find a beginner Linux book, get comfortable with some basic sys admin tasks, and then return here to dive deeper.

The Linux landscape is vast. In other books, the topics covered here have many chapters specifically dedicated to them. This book, however, is meant to be digested in 1-2 days and to give you a firm understanding of the fundamentals, i.e., how the Linux system is working internally when you do anything on it. With that knowledge, you will be able to speak on any/most questions the interviewer throws at you and demonstrate that your understanding of the fundamentals are sound.

We therefore take a simple approach to structuring this book. Each chapter discusses one of the core components of the Linux kernel. It provides the theory, sometimes a diagram, and then a list of questions and answers covering the theory. When preparing for the interview, you should test yourself with a pen and a piece of paper to answer each question and check your answers against the answers at the end of the book. Repeating this exercise until you're answering almost everything correctly will validate that you're ready for the interview.

Introduction

Chapter 1 covers interrupts. The Linux OS is event-driven, and interrupts are one of the primary sources of events that drive what happens in the OS.

Chapter 2 covers system calls. System calls are a special type of interrupts, which is why we cover them straight after the chapter on interrupts. It provides a way for user programs to access system resources through interfaces provided by the Linux kernel.

Chapter 3 covers processes. Processes are one of the core logical entities or abstractions provided by the Linux kernel. They are instances of the program being executed, which is what we use our systems for.

Chapter 4 covers memory management. Memory is one of the primary hardware resources managed by the Linux kernel, and it's important to understand how the kernel abstracts this hardware resource to be shared among all of the running processes on the system.

Chapter 5 dives deeper into how processes can manage their memory by resizing their heap and stack, and the system/library calls involved.

Chapter 6 covers signals, which are another source of events in the system used for interprocess communication.

Chapter 7 covers process scheduling and explains how the kernel gives each process a turn to run on the CPU, the different process states as they're getting scheduled, and how to influence the priority of a process getting scheduled.

Chapter 8 introduces the Linux IO model, as it provides the foundational concepts needed to introduce the other hardware resource managed by the kernel, i.e., disk storage. It explains things like file descriptors and system calls used by processes to interact with files.

Chapter 9 covers file systems by illustrating how the ext2 file system is implemented.

Chapter 10 briefly covers sockets. This is the last hardware resource we cover that is managed by the Linux kernel, namely networking. It covers the system calls used to manage sockets, and the different types of sockets that exist in Linux.

Chapter 11 gives a high-level overview of the Linux boot process.

Chapter 12 covers a more sysadmin part of Linux: troubleshooting. We attempt to convey a general approach to troubleshooting Linux systems. This chapter is included because Linux system troubleshooting is also covered in the Linux interviews.

Chapter 1: Interrupts

An operating system (OS) interrupt is a signal that the OS receives from either hardware or software. Interrupts allow the OS to stop the current process and switch to another process to handle the interrupt request.

How Interrupts Work

Interrupt Request (IRQ): When a hardware device needs to communicate with the CPU or the OS, it sends an IRQ to the CPU. The IRQ is usually sent through an interrupt line on the motherboard or the system bus.

Interrupt Handler: Once the CPU receives an IRQ, it stops the current process and transfers control to an Interrupt Handler routine in the OS. The Interrupt Handler routine is responsible for servicing the interrupt and determining what action needs to be taken.

Interrupt Service Routine (ISR): The Interrupt Handler routine typically calls an ISR to handle the interrupt request. The ISR is a specific routine that is designed to handle a particular type of interrupt. For example, a keyboard ISR might handle keyboard input, while a disk drive ISR might handle data transfer.

NOTE: *Interrupt Handlers and ISRs are often used interchangeably, but there is a subtle difference between them. An Interrupt Handler is a piece of code that manages the overall interrupt handling process. It receives an interrupt request and performs some basic processing, such as acknowledging the interrupt, saving the context of the interrupted program, and dispatching control to the appropriate ISR. An ISR, on the other hand, is a specific function responsible for handling a particular type of interrupt. The Interrupt Handler calls the appropriate ISR based on the type of interrupt received. The ISR then performs the specific processing required to handle that interrupt, such as reading data from a hardware device, updating data structures in memory, or sending data to an output device.*

Interrupt Masking: The OS uses a mechanism called Interrupt Masking to prioritize Interrupt Requests as a way of preventing interrupts from interfering with critical OS tasks. When an interrupt occurs, the OS can choose to mask the interrupt and handle it later when it is more convenient.

Interrupt Nesting: This is a feature that allows multiple interrupts to occur at the same time. When an interrupt occurs while the CPU is already servicing another interrupt, the CPU saves the current state and starts servicing the new interrupt. Once the new interrupt is handled, the CPU returns to the previous interrupt and continues where it left off.

Interrupt Vector Table (IVT): This is a data structure in the OS that contains information about each interrupt request. The IVT is used by the Interrupt Handler routine to determine which ISR to call when an interrupt occurs.

Return from Interrupt: Once the ISR has completed its task, it returns control back to the Interrupt Handler routine. The Interrupt Handler routine then restores the saved state of the interrupted process and resumes its execution.

Overall, OS interrupts are essential mechanisms that allow hardware devices and software processes to communicate with the OS and each other. By using interrupts, the OS can manage multiple tasks and respond quickly to events without wasting CPU resources.

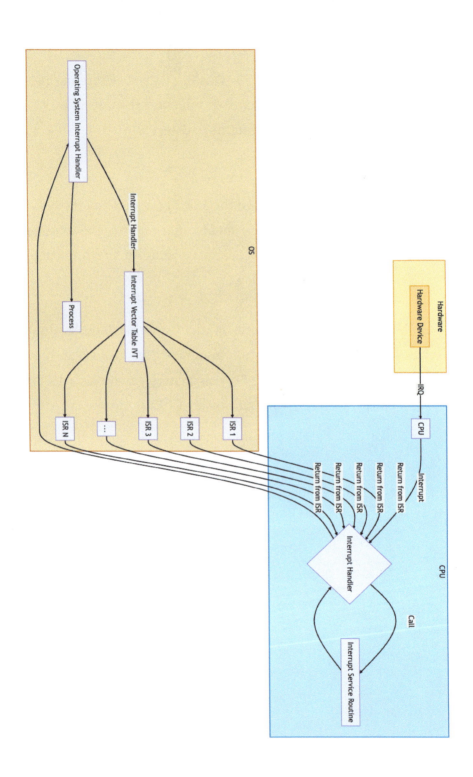

14

The diagram illustrates the flow of interrupts in a system, involving the hardware, CPU, and OS components:

- The "Hardware Device" represents a device such as a keyboard.
- The "CPU" represents the central processing unit.
- The "Interrupt Handler" is a component in the CPU that manages interrupt handling.
- The "IRS" is a specific routine that handles a particular type of interrupt.

The flow of interrupts is as follows:

1. The "Hardware Device" sends an IRQ to the CPU.
2. The "CPU" receives the IRQ and transfers control to the "Interrupt Handler."
3. The "Interrupt Handler" calls the appropriate "ISR" based on the interrupt type.
4. The "ISR" performs specific processing related to the interrupt, such as reading data or updating data structures.
5. Once the ISR completes its task, it returns control to the "Interrupt Handler."
6. The "Interrupt Handler" then resumes the interrupted process, which could be a "Process" like a text editor.

The "Operating System" also plays a role in interrupt handling:

- The "Operating System Interrupt Handler" manages the overall interrupt handling process in the OS.
- The "IVT" is a data structure in the OS that contains information about each interrupt request and their corresponding ISRs.
- The IVT is consulted by the "Interrupt Handler" to determine which ISR to call based on the interrupt type.

Questions

1. What is an OS interrupt?
2. What is an IRQ?
3. What is an Interrupt Handler?
4. What is an Interrupt Service Routine (ISR)?
5. What is Interrupt Masking?
6. What is Interrupt Nesting?
7. What is the Interrupt Vector Table (IVT)?
8. How does an ISR return control back to the Interrupt Handler routine?
9. How do interrupts help the OS manage multiple tasks?
10. Why are OS interrupts important?

Chapter 2: System Calls

Before we dive into system calls, we establish a brief understanding around the privilege levels of the Linux OS.

Access Rings

The Linux kernel has two main access rings: Ring 0 (also known as kernel mode) and Ring 3 (also known as user mode). In Ring 0, the kernel and device drivers have the highest level of privilege and access to system resources. This includes direct access to hardware, memory management, and scheduling. The kernel operates in Ring 0 at all times and handles all system tasks. In Ring 3, user applications and processes run with limited access to system resources. In this mode, applications can only access system resources through system calls, which are mediated by the kernel. This provides a layer of protection between user applications and system resources, preventing malicious or buggy applications from causing harm to the system.

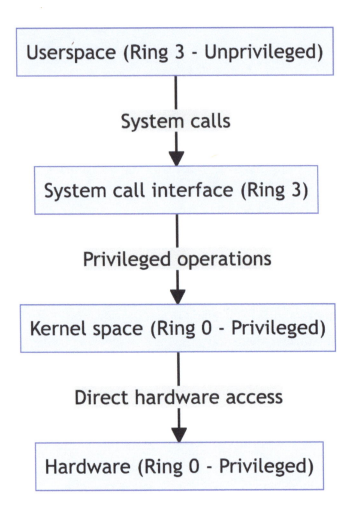

In this diagram, the ring numbers range from 0 to 3, with lower numbers representing higher levels of privilege and access to system resources. The highest privilege level is 0, which is reserved for the most sensitive system operations and is only accessible by the kernel and device drivers. The lowest privilege level is 3, which is used by user applications and processes and has the most limited access to system resources.

System Calls

In Linux, system calls are a way for user-space programs to request services from the kernel. They provide a standardized interface between user-space and kernel-space, allowing programs to perform privileged operations such as creating or deleting files, allocating memory, and accessing hardware resources.

How System Calls Work

A user-space program calls a function from a library, such as the C standard library. This function typically wraps a system call, providing a more convenient interface for the program to use.

The library function places arguments for the system call into registers or on the stack, depending on the calling convention for the corresponding architecture. These arguments specify the desired operation and any required parameters.

The library function executes a special instruction, such as the assembly instruction for x86 architecture CPUs INT 0x80, that generates a software interrupt and transfers control to the kernel. The processor responds by performing a context switch, where the processor switches from user mode to kernel mode by stopping the current program and switching to the interrupt handler. This involves saving the current state of the processor, including the program counter, registers, and other relevant data.

The interrupt handler in the kernel checks the interrupt number to determine which interrupt was generated. In the case of a software interrupt, the interrupt number corresponds to the system call number that was requested. The interrupt handler determines which system call was requested by examining the value in a register or memory location. This value corresponds to a unique number for each system call, known as a syscall number.

The kernel verifies the arguments passed by the user-space program, ensuring they are valid and don't pose a security risk. This involves copying data from user space to kernel space, where the kernel can access it directly.

The kernel performs the requested operation on behalf of the user-space program. This may involve accessing hardware resources, modifying the file system, or allocating memory.

The kernel returns control to the user-space program by transferring execution back to the library function. This also involves a context switch from kernel mode to user mode.

The library function returns the result of the system call to the user-space program. This typically involves placing the result in a register or memory location that the program can access.

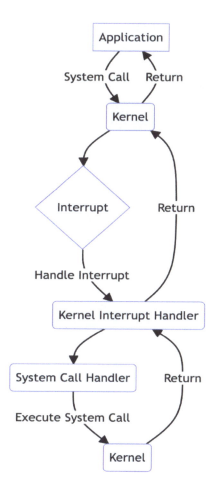

In this diagram, the application triggers a software interrupt to make a system call. The interrupt handler in the kernel takes over and transfers control to the system call handler, which executes the requested operation and returns control to the interrupt handler. The interrupt handler then returns control to the application, and the system call is complete. During the system call, the CPU switches from user mode to kernel mode to allow the kernel to execute privileged instructions.

Common System Calls

open() and close(): These system calls are used to open and close files or other resources. The open system call takes a filename and flags as input, and returns a file descriptor that can be used for subsequent read and write operations. The close system call is used to release the resources associated with a file descriptor.

```
int open(const char *pathname, int flags, mode_t mode);
```

```
int close(int fd);
```

The first argument *pathname* is the path to the file to be opened. The second argument specifies how the file should be opened, such as for reading, writing, or both, and whether to create the file if it doesn't exist. The third argument mode specifies the permissions to set on the file if it is created.

The open system call returns a non-negative file descriptor on success and -1 on error.

The close system call is used to close a file that was previously opened using open. The only argument *fd* is the file descriptor of the file to be closed. The close system call returns 0 on success and -1 on error. If an error occurs, errno is set to indicate the specific error that occurred.

read() and write(): These system calls are used to read and write data to a file or other resource. The read system call takes a file descriptor, a buffer, and a length as input, and returns the number of bytes read. The write system call takes a file descriptor, a buffer, and a length as input, and writes the data to the file.

ssize_t read(int fd, void *buf, size_t count);

ssize_t write(int fd, const void *buf, size_t count);

In both cases, the first argument *fd* is the file descriptor of the file or device to read from or write to. The second argument *buf* is a pointer to a buffer where the data read or written will be stored. The third argument *count* is the maximum number of bytes to read or write.

The read system call returns the number of bytes actually read, which may be less than count if the end of the file is reached or an error occurs. The write system call returns the number of bytes actually written, which may be less than count if an error occurs. If an error occurs, both read and write return -1 and set the global *errno* variable to indicate the specific error that occurred.

fork() and exec(): These system calls are used to create new processes. The fork system call creates a new process that is a copy of the parent process, while the exec system call replaces the current process with a new process image.

pid_t fork(void);

int execve(const char *filename, char *const argv[], char *const envp[]);

The fork system call creates a new process by duplicating the calling process. The new process, known as the child process, is an exact copy of the parent process, with the same program code and data. After the fork system call, both the parent and child processes continue executing from the instruction following the fork call. The fork system call returns the Process ID (PID) of the child process in the parent process, or 0 in the child process, or -1 on error.

The execve system call is used to replace the current (child) process with a new process. The new process is specified by the *filename* argument, which is the path to the executable file to be executed, and the *argv* and *envp* arguments, which are arrays of strings containing the command-line arguments and environment variables to be passed to the new process. The execve system call does not return on success, but returns -1 on error. If an error occurs, *errno* is set to indicate the specific error that occurred.

It's worth noting that fork and execve are often used together in sequence to create a new child process and then replace it with a different program.

getpid() and getppid(): These system calls are used to get the PID and PID of the current process.

```
pid_t getpid(void);
```

```
pid_t getppid(void);
```

The getpid system call returns the PID of the calling process. There are no arguments to this function.

The getppid system call returns the PID of the parent of the calling process. There are no arguments to this function.

Both of these system calls return a non-negative PID on success and -1 on error. If an error occurs, *errno* is set to indicate the specific error that occurred.

socket() and connect(): These system calls are used for networking. The socket system call creates a new socket, while the connect system call connects to a remote host.

```
int socket(int domain, int type, int protocol);
```

```
int connect(int sockfd, const struct sockaddr *addr, socklen_t
addrlen);
```

The socket system call creates a new socket and returns a file descriptor that can be used to read from or write to the socket. The *domain* argument specifies the protocol family to be used, such as AF_INET for IPv4 or AF_INET6 for IPv6. The *type* argument specifies the type of socket to be created, such as SOCK_STREAM for a TCP socket or SOCK_DGRAM for a UDP socket. The *protocol* argument specifies the protocol to be used, such as IPPROTO_TCP for TCP or IPPROTO_UDP for UDP.

The socket system call returns a non-negative file descriptor on success and -1 on error.

The connect system call is used to establish a connection to a remote socket. The *sockfd* argument is the file descriptor returned by the socket system call. The *addr* argument is a pointer to a sockaddr structure that contains the address of the remote socket. The *addrlen* argument is the length of that sockaddr structure.

The connect system call returns 0 on success and -1 on error. If an error occurs, *errno* is set to indicate the specific error that occurred.

It's worth noting that there are many other system calls and library functions involved in network programming, such as bind, listen, accept, send, and recv.

exit() and wait(): The exit system call is used by a child process to terminate the current process and return a status code to the parent process. The wait system call is used by a parent process to wait for a child process to terminate.

```
void exit(int status);
```

```
pid_t wait(int *status);
```

The exit system call terminates the calling process and returns a status code to the parent process. The *status* argument is an integer value passed to the parent process to indicate the reason for the process termination. The exit system call does not return.

The wait system call is used by a parent process to wait for a child process to terminate. If the child process has already terminated, the wait system call returns immediately with the child's exit status. If the child process has not yet terminated, the wait system call blocks until the child process terminates. The *status* argument is a pointer to the integer where the exit status of the child process will be stored.

The wait system call returns the PID of the terminated child process, or -1 on error. If an error occurs, *errno* is set to indicate the specific error that occurred.

Linux Commands to Inspect System Calls

There are several available Linux commands to inspect system calls:

strace: This is probably the most common command, used to trace system calls and signals made by a process. It can be used to diagnose issues with programs by analyzing the system calls they make. To use strace, simply run the command followed by the name of the program you want to trace.
For example:

```
strace ls
```

This will run the "ls" command and display all the system calls it makes.

ltrace: This command is used to trace library calls made by a process. It can be used to diagnose issues with programs by analyzing the library calls they make. To use ltrace, simply run the command followed by the name of the program you want to trace.

For example:

```
ltrace ls
```

This will run the "ls" command and display all the library calls it makes.

ftrace: This is a kernel-level tracer that can be used to trace system calls made by all processes on the system. It can be used to diagnose system-level issues by analyzing the system calls made by different processes. To use ftrace, you'll need to enable it in the kernel configuration and then use command-line tools to control the tracing.

For example:

```
echo syscalls > /sys/kernel/debug/tracing/current_tracer
```

This will enable tracing of system calls. You can then use the "cat" command to view the trace output:

```
cat /sys/kernel/debug/tracing/trace
```

strace-ng: This is a more advanced version of strace to trace system calls made by multiple threads and processes simultaneously. It can be useful for analyzing complex multi-threaded programs. To use strace-ng, simply run the command followed by the name of the program you want to trace.

For example:

```
strace-ng -p 1234
```

This will trace the system calls made by the process with PID 1234.

These commands can be very helpful for debugging and analyzing programs that make system calls in the Linux kernel.

Questions

1. What are system calls?

2. Why are system calls important?

3. What happens when an application makes a system call?

4. How are system calls implemented in Linux?

5. What is the purpose of the system call table?

6. What is the difference between a system call and a library call?

7. What is strace?

8. What is ltrace?

9. What is ftrace?

10. What is the difference between strace and ltrace?

11. What is the difference between strace and ftrace?

12. What are some common system calls used by all programs?

13. What is the purpose of the open() system call?

14. What is the purpose of the fork() system call?

Chapter 3: Processes

Overview

In the Linux kernel, a process is an instance of a program in execution. It is an independent entity that has its own memory space, program counter, stack, and set of resources such as open files and network connections.

Each process in Linux has a unique PID, which is used to identify and manage that process. The Linux kernel creates a new process when a user initiates a program or executes a command, and the process runs in its own virtual address space.

The Linux kernel uses a scheduler to manage the execution of processes. The scheduler determines which process to run next based on a set of scheduling policies and priorities. The scheduler also ensures that each process is given a fair share of CPU time and that high-priority processes are executed before low-priority ones.

Processes in Linux can communicate with each other using various IPC mechanisms, such as pipes, sockets, shared memory, and signals. This allows processes to exchange data and synchronize.

Internal Structure

Process State:

The process state represents the current state of the process. It can be one of several states, such as running, sleeping, waiting, or stopped.

Memory Layout:

The memory layout describes the virtual address space of the process. It includes areas such as the text segment (containing the executable code), the data segment (containing initialized data), the BSS segment (containing uninitialized data), and the heap and stack segments.

File Descriptors:

The file descriptors represent the files or other resources that the process has open. Each file descriptor has an associated file table entry that describes the file's state and location.

Scheduling Information:

The scheduling information includes the process's priority, scheduling policy, and other parameters that affect how the process is scheduled.

Signal Handlers:

Signal handlers are functions executed in response to signals received by the process. The task_struct structure contains a list of signal handlers that the process has registered.

Parent and Child Process IDs:

Each process has a Parent Process ID (PPID) that identifies its parent process, as well as one or more child PID that identify its child processes.

```
+-----------------------------------------------+
|                  task_struct                  |
|-----------------------------------------------|
|  PID          |        process ID             |
|-----------------------------------------------|
|  PPID         |        parent process ID       |
|-----------------------------------------------|
|  state        |        process state          |
|-----------------------------------------------|
|  priority     |        scheduling priority     |
|-----------------------------------------------|
|  flags        |        process flags          |
|-----------------------------------------------|
|  mm           |        memory management       |
|-----------------------------------------------|
|  files        |        open file descriptors   |
|-----------------------------------------------|
|  signal       |        signal handling         |
|-----------------------------------------------|
|  sigset       |        signal mask            |
|-----------------------------------------------|
|  exit_code    |        exit status            |
|-----------------------------------------------|
|  children     |        child processes         |
|-----------------------------------------------|
|  siblings     |        sibling processes        |
|-----------------------------------------------|
|  parent       |        parent process          |
|-----------------------------------------------|
|  utime        |        user CPU time            |
|-----------------------------------------------|
|  stime        |        system CPU time          |
|-----------------------------------------------|
|  start_time   |        start time             |
|-----------------------------------------------|
|  cgroup       |        control group           |
|-----------------------------------------------|
```

These are just a few of the key elements of the task_struct structure.

Process Memory Layout

In a Linux process, memory is divided into several segments, each serving a different purpose:

- **Text segment**: This segment contains the executable code of the process. It is read-only and shared among all processes that use the same executable code.
- **Data segment (initialized)**: This segment contains the global and static variables used by the process. It is typically read-write and initialized at program startup.
- **BSS segment (uninitialized)**: This segment contains the uninitialized data for the process e.g., uninitialized global and static variables. It is typically read-write and initialized to zero at program startup.
- **Heap segment**: This segment is used for dynamic memory allocation. It is typically read-write and grows upward in memory as the process requests more memory.
- **Stack segment**: This segment is used to store local variables and function calls during program execution. It is typically read-write and grows downward in memory as the process pushes more data onto the stack.
- **Memory-mapped files segment**: This segment is used for memory-mapped files, which allows files to be accessed as if they were part of the process's memory. It is typically read-write and can be shared among multiple processes.

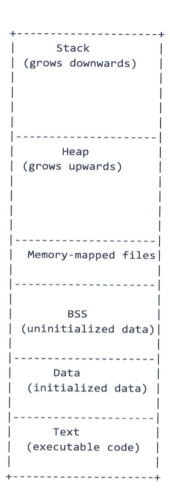

```
+-------------------------+
|          Stack          |
|     (grows downwards)   |
|                         |
|                         |
|                         |
|-------------------------|
|          Heap           |
|     (grows upwards)     |
|                         |
|                         |
|                         |
|-------------------------|
|   Memory-mapped files   |
|                         |
|-------------------------|
|           BSS           |
|    (uninitialized data) |
|                         |
|-------------------------|
|          Data           |
|    (initialized data)   |
|                         |
|-------------------------|
|          Text           |
|    (executable code)    |
|                         |
+-------------------------+
```

Process Lifecycle

The lifecycle of a process can be divided into several stages, each of
which involves different system calls. Here's an overview:

Process Creation:

The first stage in the lifecycle of a process is process creation. This
involves using a system call like fork() or clone() to create a new
process. The fork() system call creates a copy of the current process,

while the clone() system call creates a new process with shared resources.

Executing the Program:

After a process has been created, the next stage is to execute the program. This involves using a system call like exec() to replace the current process's memory space with a new program. The new program is loaded into memory and its main() function is executed. The parent process calls the wait() system call to receive the exit status of the child process and clean up the child resources.

Process Termination:

The final stage in the lifecycle of a process is process termination. This involves using a system call like exit() to terminate the current process. The exit() system call performs various cleanup tasks, including closing open files and releasing memory.

Process Suspension and Resumption:

During its lifetime, a process may be suspended and resumed by the kernel. System calls that manage the process's state include wait(), waitpid(), and kill(). The wait() system call suspends the current process until a child process terminates, while the kill() system call sends a signal to a process to request that it is suspended or terminated.

Interprocess Communication (IPC):

Processes can communicate with each other using system calls like pipe(), socket(), and mmap(). These system calls provide various mechanisms for processes to exchange data and synchronize.

Zombie & Orphan Process

In Linux, a zombie process and an orphan process are two different concepts related to the lifecycle of processes:

A zombie process is a process that has completed execution but still has an entry in the process table. This happens when a parent process fails to call the wait() system call to collect the exit status of its terminated child process. As a result, the terminated child process becomes a zombie process, and its resources are not fully released until the parent process collects its exit status by calling wait() or waitpid(). Zombie processes do not consume any CPU time, but they do consume system memory and can eventually cause the system to run out of process table entries. To prevent this, it is important for parent processes to properly manage their child processes by calling wait() or waitpid().

In Linux, you can find zombie processes using the "ps" command with the "aux" option:

- Open a terminal window.
- Type ps aux and press Enter.
- Look for any processes with a "Z" in the STAT column. The "Z" indicates that the process is a zombie.
- Note the PID of the zombie process. This will be listed in the second column of the output.
- If you want to terminate the zombie process, you can use the "kill" command with the respective PID. For example, "kill 1234" will send a signal to process 1234 to terminate.

It is important to note that killing a zombie process will not have any effect on the system, as the process has already completed execution and is simply waiting for its parent process to collect its exit status. To prevent zombie processes from accumulating, parent processes must properly manage their child processes by calling wait() or waitpid() to collect their exit status.

An orphan process is a process that is still running but has lost its parent process. This happens when the parent process terminates before the child process. Subsequently, the child process becomes an orphan process and is inherited by the init process (PID 1), which becomes its new parent. The init process periodically checks for orphan processes and collects their exit status by calling wait() or waitpid().

Questions

1. What is a zombie process?
2. How does a process become a zombie?
3. How can you find a zombie process?
4. Can a zombie process consume system memory?
5. Can a zombie process consume CPU time?
6. How can you terminate a zombie process?
7. What is an orphan process?
8. How does a process become an orphan?
9. What happens to an orphan process?
10. What system call is used to create a new process in Linux?
11. What is the exec() system call in Linux?
12. How can you get the PID of the current process in Linux?
13. What system call is used to wait for a child process to terminate in Linux?
14. What system call is used to change the priority of a process in Linux?
15. What system call is used to terminate a process in Linux?

Chapter 4: Memory Management

When a process is created in Linux, it is given its own virtual address space, which is a range of memory addresses that the process can use. This virtual address space is divided into small chunks called pages, which are typically 4KB in size. Physical RAM is also divided up into small chunks of the same size called page frames. Each page frame is given a unique virtual address, and the process can access the contents of that page frame by using that address.

The virtual addresses used by the process are not the same as the physical addresses used by the computer's memory hardware. Instead, the Linux kernel uses a page table to map virtual addresses to physical addresses. Page tables are data structures that contain information about the virtual-to-physical address mappings for each page in the process's address space.

When the process tries to access the contents of a page, the CPU generates a virtual memory address. The Linux kernel uses the page table to look up the physical address corresponding to that virtual address, and then the CPU can access the contents of the page at the physical address.

The page table is stored in memory, and it can become quite large for processes that use a lot of memory. To optimize performance, the

Linux kernel uses a technique called "paging" to move pages between memory and disk. Pages that are not currently being used by the process can be moved to disk, freeing up physical memory for other processes to use. When the process needs to access a page that is not currently in memory, the Linux kernel then loads it back into physical memory from disk.

To keep track of which pages have been modified since they were last loaded from disk, the Linux kernel uses a "dirty bit" for each page. When the process modifies the contents of a page, the dirty bit is set to indicate that the page has been changed. When the Linux kernel needs to move a page from memory to disk, it checks the dirty bit to see if the page needs to be written back to disk first.

Memory Management Unit (MMU)

The MMU is a hardware component in the CPU that plays a crucial role in the memory management of a process in the Linux kernel. The MMU translates virtual addresses used by the process into physical addresses used by the hardware. When a process attempts to access a page that is not currently in physical memory, the MMU generates a "page fault" exception. A page fault is an interrupt (see chapter 1 regarding interrupts) raised by the MMU to signal to the Linux kernel that the process is attempting to access a page that is not currently in physical memory. At this point, the kernel must handle the page fault by bringing the missing page into physical memory and updating the page table to reflect the new mapping.

The Linux kernel handles page faults using the page fault handler, a section of code that is executed when a page fault occurs. This determines the cause of the page fault and takes the appropriate action to resolve it. If the missing page is found in the page cache (i.e., the portion of the kernel's memory used to store frequently accessed files or file data) or swap space (i.e., the designated area of the disk where the kernel stores pages of memory that are not currently used by processes), the kernel will load it into physical memory and update the page table.

The MMU and the page fault mechanism enable the Linux kernel to provide virtual memory to processes. This enables processes to access more memory than is physically available by storing some memory pages on disk and only loading them into physical memory when they are needed. This can improve the overall performance of the system by allowing more processes to run simultaneously without running out of physical memory.

```
PROCESS VIRTUAL MEMORY                    PHYSICAL MEMORY
+------------------+            +------------------+
|                  |            |                  |
|      Code        |            |      Code        |
|                  |            |                  |
|------------------|            |------------------|
|                  |            |                  |
|      Data        |            |      Data        |
|                  |            |                  |
|------------------| PAGE TABLE |------------------|
|                  | ---------> | Page Table       |
|      Heap        |            | (stored in phys  ||
|                  |            | memory)          |
|------------------|            |                  |
|                  |            |                  |
|      Stack       |            |                  |
|                  |            |                  |
|------------------|            |                  |
|                  |            |                  |
|      Shared      |            |                  |
|      Libraries   |            |                  |
|                  |            |                  |
+------------------+            +------------------+

PAGE TABLE
+--------------+-------+-------+--------+-------+
| Page Number  | Valid | Dirty | Access | Address|
|              | Bit   | Bit   | Bits   |       |
+--------------+-------+-------+--------+-------+
|              |       |       |        |       |
|              |       |       |        |       |
|              |       |       |        |       |
|              |       |       |        |       |
|              |       |       |        |       |
+--------------+-------+-------+--------+-------+
```

In this diagram, the top section represents the virtual memory space of a process, which is divided into several sections, as described in *Process Memory Layout*. The page table is used to map the virtual addresses used by the process to the physical addresses used by the computer's memory hardware. The page table is stored in physical memory, and it contains information about which virtual pages are currently mapped to which physical pages. When the process accesses a memory location using a virtual address, the MMU uses the page table to translate the virtual address to a physical address, which is used to access the contents of the memory location in physical memory.

Questions

1. What is memory management?
2. Why is memory management important?
3. What is virtual memory?
4. What is a page table?
5. How is the dirty bit used in memory management?
6. How is memory address translation performed in Linux?
7. How is the Translation Lookaside Buffer (TLB) related to the page table?
8. What is demand paging?
9. What is a page fault?
10. What is memory swapping?
11. What is a swap file?

Chapter 5: Memory Allocation

In this chapter, we'll discuss how a process allocates memory dynamically. This is often required by a program, e.g., a user keeps inputting values to the program, and a linked list needs to keep adding nodes for each input value. To dynamically allocate memory, a program can increase the size of the heap or the stack.

A quick review of the layout of the memory segments of a process:

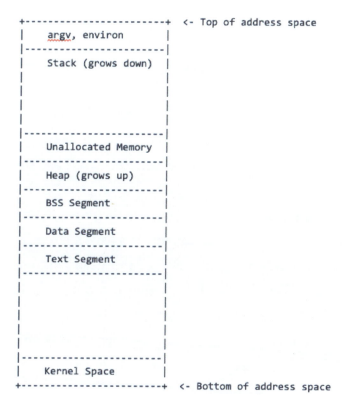

```
+-------------------------+  <- Top of address space
|     argv, environ       |
|-------------------------|
|   Stack (grows down)    |
|                         |
|                         |
|                         |
|-------------------------|
|    Unallocated Memory   |
|-------------------------|
|    Heap (grows up)      |
|-------------------------|
|   BSS Segment           |
|-------------------------|
|   Data Segment          |
|-------------------------|
|   Text Segment          |
|-------------------------|
|                         |
|                         |
|                         |
|                         |
|-------------------------|
|   Kernel Space          |
+-------------------------+  <- Bottom of address space
```

In this diagram, the *argv* and *environ* pointers are located at the top of the address space, followed by the stack segment, which grows downwards toward lower memory addresses. The unallocated memory section represents the space that is not currently being used by the process. The heap segment is located below the unallocated memory section and grows upwards toward higher memory addresses. The BSS segment, which contains uninitialized global and static variables, is located below the heap, and the data segment, which contains initialized global and static variables, is located below the BSS segment. Finally, the text segment, which contains the program's executable code, is located at the bottom of the address space.

Using the Heap

brk() and sbrk() system calls

The heap is a region of memory in a process's virtual address space that is used for dynamic memory allocation. In Linux, the heap is managed by the kernel using two system calls: brk() and sbrk().

When a program starts up, the kernel sets the program break, which is the end of the process's data segment, to a fixed address in memory. This address marks the initial end of the heap, and all memory beyond it is unallocated. The brk() system call can be used to set the program break to a new value, effectively resizing the heap. The new value must be greater than or equal to the current program break and less than or equal to the maximum size of the process's address space.

The sbrk() system call is used to increment the program break by a specified amount, effectively allocating additional memory on the heap. The value passed to sbrk() specifies the number of bytes to add to the heap, and the return value is a pointer to the start of the newly allocated memory.

Malloc and free

In addition to brk() and sbrk(), the C standard library provides a memory allocation function called malloc(). In C, this function is used to dynamically allocate memory on the heap, while the free() function is used to deallocate memory that was previously allocated by malloc().

When a program calls malloc(), the C library implementation of this function keeps track of the size and location of the allocated memory block. This information is typically stored in a data structure called the heap metadata, which is also stored on the heap. When the program is finished using the allocated memory block, it should call free() to release the memory back to the heap. When free() is called, it marks the memory block as free in the heap metadata and adds it to a free list for later reuse. If subsequent calls to malloc() request memory that can be satisfied by a block on the free list, the C library implementation will reuse that block instead of requesting new memory from the kernel with sbrk(). This can help reduce the number of system calls and improve performance.

It's important to note that calling free() does not necessarily release the memory back to the OS. Instead, the memory is returned to the heap, where it can be reused by subsequent calls to malloc(). However, it's also possible for the program to resize the heap using brk() or sbrk() to release memory back to the OS.

Using the Stack

In Linux, memory for the stack is allocated automatically when a new thread or process is created. The stack is a region of memory used to store local variables, function call information, and other data related to the execution of a program. The memory allocation for the stack is managed by the kernel.

When a new thread or process is created, the kernel reserves a contiguous block of memory for its stack. The size of this block is usually fixed and defined during the program's compilation, and it can be adjusted with compiler or system-specific options. The stack typically grows downwards from high to low memory addresses, so as functions are called and local variables are pushed onto the stack, it expands downwards.

The memory for the stack is released when the thread or process exits. The kernel automatically deallocates the stack memory, making it available for other processes or threads.

For example:

```
void my_function() {
    int x = 10; // integer variable allocated on the
stack
    char buffer[256]; // character array allocated on
the stack
    // code
}
```

Here, the integer variable x and the character array *buffer* are allocated on the stack. When my_function() is called, space is immediately reserved on the stack for these variables. When my_function() returns, the space allocated for these variables is released.

It is important to note that the stack has a limited size, and allocating too much memory on the stack can result in a stack overflow and program crash. To avoid this, large or dynamically-sized data structures should be allocated on the heap using malloc() and free().

Questions

1. What is the difference between brk() and sbrk() system calls?
2. How does the brk() system call modify the program break pointer of a process?
3. What is the purpose of the sbrk() system call in memory allocation?
4. Can the sbrk() system call allocate a continuous memory block of arbitrary size in a process' heap?
5. How does the malloc() function utilize the sbrk() system call to allocate memory on the heap?
6. What happens when a program calls the malloc() function with a size greater than the available free memory on the heap?
7. How does the free() function release memory allocated by malloc() back to the heap?
8. Can free() return memory to the OS when the released memory is at the end of the heap?
9. What happens when a program calls free() with an invalid memory address?
10. How does the free list help optimize memory allocation and deallocation in a program that uses the malloc() and free() functions?

Chapter 6: Signals

In the Linux kernel, signals are a mechanism for IPC. Signals allow a process to send a notification to another process or to itself. When a process receives a signal, it can perform a specific action, such as terminating or interrupting a system call.

Here are some important definitions/details about signals in the Linux kernel:

Signal numbers: Signals are identified by numbers which range from 1 to 64. Each signal has a specific meaning and can trigger a particular action. For example, signal 1 (SIGHUP) is typically used to request a process to reload its configuration file.

Signal handlers: When a process receives a signal, it can execute a user-defined signal handler function to handle the signal. A signal handler is a function that is registered with the kernel and executed by the process when it receives the signal. The default action for most signals is to terminate the process, but a signal handler can override this behavior.

Signal delivery: When a process receives a signal, the kernel suspends the process's execution and delivers the signal to the process. The process can then either handle the signal or defer its handling by blocking the signal until a later time.

Signal masking: A process can mask certain signals to prevent them from being delivered. When a signal is masked, the kernel will not deliver it to the process until it is unmasked again. This allows a process to avoid being interrupted by certain signals during critical operations.

Real-time signals: These are a special type of signal that allows a process to specify a data payload to be delivered along with the signal. Real-time signals are identified by numbers from 32 to 64 and can be used for high-priority communication between processes.

Common Signals

Some of the most common signals in the Linux kernel and their default action are:

SIGTERM (15): This signal is sent to a process to request it to terminate gracefully. The default action is to terminate the process.

SIGKILL (9): This signal is used to force a process to terminate immediately. The default action is to terminate the process.

SIGINT (2): This signal is sent to a process when the user types Ctrl-C in the terminal. The default action is to terminate the process.

SIGHUP (1): This signal is used to request a process when its controlling terminal is closed. The default action is to terminate the process.

SIGUSR1 (10) and SIGUSR2 (12): These signals are user-defined and can be used for any purpose. The default action is to terminate the process, but they are often handled by user-defined signal handlers.

SIGSTOP (19) and SIGTSTP (20): These signals are used to suspend a process temporarily. The default action is to stop the process.

SIGCONT (18): This signal is used to resume a stopped or suspended process. The default action is to continue the process.

These are just a few examples of the many signals available in the Linux kernel. Each signal has a specific meaning and can trigger a particular action, but these default actions can be overridden by a signal handler.

Fatal Signals

There are some signals in the Linux kernel that cannot be caught or ignored by a process. These signals are called "fatal signals" and will always result in the process being terminated. Here are the signals that cannot be handled:

SIGKILL (9): This signal is used to force a process to terminate immediately. The only way to terminate a process that is stuck in an infinite loop or unresponsive is to send it a SIGKILL signal.

SIGSTOP (19): This signal is used to suspend a process temporarily. Once a process has been stopped with SIGSTOP, it cannot be resumed until it receives a SIGCONT signal.

SIGCONT (18): This signal is used to resume a process that has been stopped or suspended. Once a process has received a SIGSTOP signal, it cannot be resumed until it receives a SIGCONT signal.

SIGBUS (7), SIGILL (4), SIGFPE (8), SIGSEGV (11), SIGSYS (31), and SIGTRAP (5): These signals are raised when a process encounters a fatal error, such as a segmentation fault or an illegal instruction. They will always result in the process being terminated.

In general, signals that are used for critical system functions, such as process management or error reporting, cannot be caught or ignored.

Signals in Action: nohup

nohup is a command that is used to run a process in the background and protect it from receiving the SIGHUP signal, which is typically sent to a process when the terminal it is attached to is closed.

When a process is started using the nohup command, it is detached from the terminal and is not associated with any controlling terminal. This means that it cannot receive the SIGHUP signal when the terminal is closed, which would normally cause the process to terminate.

Instead, the nohup command intercepts the SIGHUP signal and ignores it so that the process can continue running in the background even if the terminal is closed. This is achieved by setting the signal handler to ignore the SIGHUP signal.

Here's an example of how to use the nohup command:

```
$ nohup myscript.sh &
```

In this example, the myscript.sh script is run in the background with the nohup command. The & at the end of the command runs the script in the background and allows the terminal to be used for other commands.

By using the nohup command, the `myscript.sh` script will continue to run even if the terminal is closed, as the SIGHUP signal will be ignored. This can be useful for processes that need to continue running in the background even after the user has logged out or closed the terminal.

Procfs

Information about signals is available in the /proc filesystem in Linux. The /proc/[pid]/status file contains various status information about a process, including information about the signals that are currently being handled by the process.

Here's an example of the contents of the /proc/[pid]/status file:

```
Name:	bash
State:	S (sleeping)
Tgid:	1874
Pid:	1874
PPid:	1873
TracerPid:	0
Uid:	1000	1000	1000	1000
Gid:	1000	1000	1000	1000
FDSize:	256
Groups:	4 24 27 30 46 113 128 1000
VmPeak:	91968 kB
VmSize:	88828 kB
VmLck:	0 kB
VmPin:	0 kB
VmHWM:	11768 kB
VmRSS:	11768 kB
RssAnon:	11708 kB
RssFile:	3996 kB
RssShmem:	72 kB
VmData:	17484 kB
VmStk:	136 kB
VmExe:	796 kB
VmLib:	16660 kB
Signal:	6
SigQ:	0/5104
SigPnd:	0000000000000000
ShdPnd:	0000000000000000
SigBlk:	0000000000010000
SigIgn:	0000000000384004
SigCgt:	0000000000000000
CapInh:	0000000000000000
CapPrm:	0000000000000000
CapEff:	0000000000000000
CapBnd:	ffffffffffffffff
```

```
Cpus_allowed:    f
Cpus_allowed_list:  .   0-3
Mems_allowed:    00000000,00000001
Mems_allowed_list:      0
voluntary_ctxt_switches:        3981
nonvoluntary_ctxt_switches:     2472
```

The "Signal" field in indicates the current signal being processed by the process. In this example, the process is currently handling signal number 6.

The "SigQ" field indicates the number of signals queued for the process, while the "SigPnd" and "ShdPnd" fields indicate the signals pending for the process and shared with child processes respectively.

The "SigIgn" and "SigCgt" fields indicate the signals that are being ignored and those that are currently set to be caught by the process respectively.

The /proc/[pid]/status file can provide useful information about a process's signal handling behavior, which can be used for troubleshooting issues related to signal handling.

Questions

1. What is a signal in the context of the Linux kernel?
2. How are signals used to communicate with processes in Linux?
3. What is the difference between a synchronous and an asynchronous signal?
4. How does a process handle a signal that is sent to it?
5. What are some common signals in Linux and what are their default actions?
6. Can a process change the default action for a specific signal in Linux? If so, how?
7. What is the purpose of the kill command in Linux and how is it used to send signals to processes?
8. How does the nohup command interact with signals in Linux?
9. What is the difference between the SIGINT and SIGTERM signals?
10. Can a process ignore a signal that is sent to it in Linux? If so, how?

Chapter 7: Scheduling

Linux Scheduler

In Linux, process scheduling is handled by the kernel's scheduler. This is responsible for deciding which process should be executed on the CPU at any given time. The scheduler works by using timer interrupts generated by a hardware timer at a fixed frequency to interrupt the currently executing process and allow the scheduler to make a decision about which process should run next.

When a timer interrupt occurs, the scheduler's interrupt handler is executed. This is responsible for checking whether the currently running process has exceeded its time slice, which is a fixed amount of time that the process is allowed to run before it is preempted. If the process has exceeded its time slice, the interrupt handler preempts the process and selects a new process to run.

The scheduler uses a variety of algorithms to decide which process should run next. The most commonly used algorithm is the Completely Fair Scheduler (CFS), which is based on the idea of fair sharing of the CPU among all running processes. Under the CFS algorithm, each process is assigned a "virtual runtime" based on its priority and the amount of CPU time it has already consumed. The scheduler selects the process with the smallest virtual runtime to run next, which ensures that all processes are given a fair share of the CPU.

Other scheduling algorithms, such as the Round Robin Scheduler, are also available in Linux and can be selected based on the specific needs of the system.

In addition to timer interrupts, the scheduler is also triggered by other events, such as I/O completion or process wakeups. For example, when a process is blocked waiting for I/O, it is temporarily removed from the run queue and placed on a separate queue for blocked processes. When the I/O operation completes, the process is placed back on the run queue, and the scheduler may select it to run again.

Process scheduling in Linux is a complex and dynamic process that is critical to the efficient operation of the system. By using timer interrupts and a variety of scheduling algorithms, the Linux scheduler is able to ensure that all processes are given a fair share of the CPU and that system resources are used efficiently.

Process States

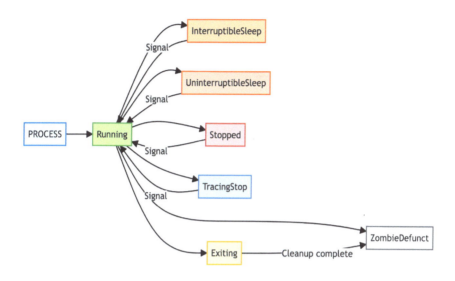

The diagram represents the different states a process can be in, using color-coded nodes and arrows to illustrate the transitions between states.

- The blue node labeled "PROCESS" represents the general process entity.
- The green node labeled "Running" represents the state where the process is actively executing on the CPU.
- The orange node labeled "InterruptibleSleep" represents the state where the process is waiting for a resource that is not immediately available but can be awakened by a signal.
- The light orange node labeled "UninterruptibleSleep" represents the state where the process is waiting for a resource that is not immediately available and cannot be interrupted by signals.

- The red node labeled "Stopped" represents the state where the process has been stopped, usually by a signal.
- The light gray node labeled "ZombieDefunct" represents the state where the process has completed execution, but its parent process has not collected its exit status yet.
- The light blue node labeled "TracingStop" represents the state where the process has been stopped for tracing purposes, usually by a debugger.
- The yellow node labeled "Exiting" represents the state where the process is waiting for its resources to be cleaned up before it is removed from the system.

The arrows indicate the possible transitions between states. For example, a process in the "Running" state can transition to the "InterruptibleSleep," "UninterruptibleSleep," "Stopped," "ZombieDefunct," "TracingStop," or "Exiting" state based on different events or signals. Similarly, processes in other states can transition back to the "Running" state upon receiving specific signals.

Signals and States

A process can be in any state and can receive signals, except for the Stopped state (T or W state in some versions of `ps` output) and the Traced state (*t* state in some versions of ps output).

When a process is stopped (e.g., by pressing CTRL-Z in the terminal), it is suspended and cannot execute any further instructions until it is resumed. While in the Stopped state, the process cannot receive any signals.

Similarly, when a process is being traced by another process (e.g., using the ptrace() system call), it is in the Traced state and cannot receive any signals until the tracing process releases it.

In all other states (e.g., Running, Sleeping, Waiting), a process can receive signals and handle them according to its signal handlers.

Changing Priority

The `nice` command is used to adjust the priority of a process. It is a utility that allows users to set the priority of a process when it is launched or change the priority of an already running process. The priority of a process is determined by its niceness value, which is a value ranging from -20 to 19.

A process with a lower niceness value will have a higher priority and will be scheduled to run before other processes with a higher niceness value. By default, all processes have a niceness value of 0.

To modify the niceness value of a process, you can use the `nice` command followed by the command you want to run. For example, to start a new process with a niceness value of 10, you can use the following command:

```
nice -n 10 <command>
```

where *<command>* is the command you want to run.

To change the niceness value of an already running process, you can use the `renice` command followed by the PID and the new niceness value. For example, to change the niceness value of a process with PID 1234 to 5, you can use the following command:

```
renice -n 5 -p 1234
```

To check the niceness value of a process, you can use the `ps` command with the `-o` option to display the niceness value in the output. For example, to display the niceness value of all processes, you can use the following command:

```
ps -eo pid,ni,cmd
```

In the output, the ni column shows the niceness value of each process. The `nice` and `renice` commands can be used by the system administrator or by users with sufficient privileges. However, users can only increase the priority of their own processes or decrease the priority of processes with a lower priority. They cannot increase the priority of processes owned by other users.

Questions

1. What is the purpose of process scheduling in Linux?
2. How does the Linux scheduler decide which process to run next?
3. What are the different states a process can be in and how do they relate to scheduling?
4. Can a process receive signals in any state? If not, which states prevent a process from receiving signals?
5. How does the nice command affect process scheduling in Linux?
6. What is the default niceness value for a process and how does it affect scheduling?
7. How can you check the niceness value of a running process in Linux?
8. How can you change the niceness value of a running process in Linux?
9. What is a signal in Linux and how is it used to communicate with a process?
10. How does a process handle signals in Linux?
11. What is the difference between a synchronous and asynchronous signal in Linux?
12. Can a process ignore a signal in Linux? If so, how?
13. What is the difference between a signal handler and a signal mask in Linux?
14. How does process scheduling in Linux relate to interrupt handling and timers?
15. Can you explain how process scheduling works in Linux, including the role of the run queue and blocked queue?

Chapter 8: Linux I/O Model

Overview

The Universal I/O Model is a key component of the Linux kernel, which provides a standardized and efficient way of handling input and output operations across different types of devices. The main goal of the Universal I/O Model is to abstract the underlying hardware details of the various devices and provide a uniform interface for application programs to interact with them.

In the Linux kernel, the Universal I/O Model is implemented using a layered approach, where the various layers communicate with each other to perform the input and output operations. The following are the main layers involved in the Universal I/O Model:

- **User space**: This layer contains the application programs that use the input/output operations. The application programs use the standard input/output functions provided by the C library, such as fread() and fwrite(), to communicate with the universal I/O subsystem.
- **Virtual file system (VFS)**: This layer provides a uniform interface to the various file systems supported by the Linux kernel. The VFS layer intercepts the input/output operations

initiated by the application programs and routes them to the appropriate file system.

- **File system**: This layer handles the input/output operations for a specific file system, such as ext4 or NTFS. The file system layer communicates with the appropriate device driver to perform the input/output operations on the physical device.
- **Device driver**: This layer provides the interface between the kernel and the physical device. The device driver translates the input/output requests into commands that are understood by the hardware.
- **Hardware**: This layer represents the physical device that is being accessed.
- When an application program initiates an input/output operation, the Universal I/O Model follows this layered approach to perform the operation. The VFS layer intercepts the operation and identifies the appropriate file system, which in turn communicates with the device driver. The device driver then sends the appropriate commands to the hardware to perform the operation.

Advantages

The Universal I/O Model provides several advantages, including:

Uniform interface: The model provides a uniform interface for application programs to interact with different types of devices. This simplifies the development of applications that need to access multiple devices.

Efficient performance: The model provides efficient performance by minimizing the number of context switches between the kernel and user space. This reduces overhead and improves the overall system performance.

Device independence: The model abstracts the hardware details of the devices, which allows applications to be developed without any dependencies on specific devices. This makes it easier to port applications across different platforms.

Overall, the Universal I/O Model is a key component of the Linux kernel that provides a standardized and efficient way of handling input and output operations across different types of devices.

Systems Calls

The Universal I/O Model in Linux uses several system calls to perform input and output operations. The following are some of the most commonly used:

open(): This system call is used to open a file or a device for input/output operations. The open() system call takes a filename and a set of flags as arguments and returns a file descriptor that can be used in subsequent input/output operations.

read(): This system call is used to read data from a file or a device. The read() system call takes a file descriptor, a buffer, and a size as arguments and returns the number of bytes read.

write(): This system call is used to write data to a file or a device. The write() system call takes a file descriptor, a buffer, and a size as arguments and returns the number of bytes written.

ioctl(): This system call is used to perform device-specific input/output operations. The ioctl() system call takes a file descriptor, an operation code, and a pointer to a data structure as arguments.

close(): This system call is used to close a file or a device that was opened using the open() system call. The close() system call takes a file descriptor as an argument.

These system calls are used by the various layers in the Universal I/O Model to perform input/output operations on different types of devices. For example, the open(), read(), write(), and close() system calls are used by the file system layer to interact with different types of file systems, while the ioctl() system call is used by the device driver layer to perform device-specific input/output operations.

File Descriptors

A file descriptor is a non-negative integer used by the OS to uniquely represent a file, a device, or a network socket that an application program can read from or write to.

In Unix-like OSs, including Linux, file descriptors are used extensively to represent input/output resources. A file descriptor is created when a file or a device is opened by an application program and is then used to read from or write to the file or device.

The following are some key aspects of file descriptors:

Uniqueness: Every file descriptor is a unique integer assigned by the OS to an open file or device. No two file descriptors can represent the same resource.

Inheritance: When a new process is created, it inherits the file descriptors of its parent process. This allows a child process to use the same files and devices as its parent process.

Standard file descriptors: Unix-like OSs define three standard file descriptors: 0 for standard input (stdin), 1 for standard output (stdout), and 2 for standard error (stderr). These file descriptors are reserved and are automatically created by the OS when a new process is started.

Limits: OSs impose limits on the number of file descriptors that a process can have at any given time. This limit can be increased by the process, subject to system-wide limits.

Manipulation: An application program can manipulate file descriptors using the dup(), dup2(), and fcntl() system calls. These system calls allow a process to duplicate a file descriptor or change its properties respectively.

File descriptors play a key role in the input/output operations of a Unix-like OS. They are used by the OS to track open files and devices and to allow application programs to read from and write to them. Understanding file descriptors is essential for programming in Unix-like environments, as it provides a way to interact with files, devices, and network sockets in a standardized and consistent manner.

How Processes Use File Descriptors

In a Unix-like operating system, including Linux, every process has its own set of file descriptors, which represent the open files, devices, and network sockets that the process is currently using.

The kernel also maintains an open file table, which is a data structure that keeps track of all open files in the system, along with their associated metadata, such as the file position, access mode, and status flags.

When a process opens a file or a device using the open() system call, the kernel creates a new entry in the open file table and assigns a unique file descriptor to that process. The file descriptor number selected is the lowest available non-negative integer that is not already in use by the process. The file descriptor is used by the process to identify the file or device in subsequent input/output operations.

The open file table maintains a reference count for each open file, which keeps track of how many processes are currently using the file. When a process closes a file using the close() system call, the kernel decrements the reference count for the file in the open file table. If the reference count reaches zero, the kernel removes the file from the open file table, freeing up system resources.

The entries in the open file table typically point to the inode entries in the inode table. The inode (index node) is a data structure in Unix-like file systems that contains metadata about a file, such as file type, permissions, timestamps, and pointers to the data blocks that hold the actual content of the file. We'll discuss the inode table in more detail in the next chapter on file systems.

When a process reads from or writes to an open file or device, the kernel uses the file descriptor to locate the corresponding entry in the open file table and performs the input/output operation on the file's data. The kernel also updates the file position in the open file table to reflect the new position of the file after the read/write operation is complete.

System Call Examples

System calls such as lseek() and dup() are used to manipulate file descriptors and the open file table.

lseek() system call:
When a process reads from or writes to an open file or device, it maintains a file offset that specifies the current position in the file. The lseek() system call is used to change the current position of the file offset associated with a specific file descriptor. This is done by allowing the process to set the file offset to a specific location in the file, or to seek a certain distance from the current position.

In the open file table, the file offset is stored with other metadata for the file, such as the access mode and status flags. When a process calls lseek() with a file descriptor, the kernel uses the file descriptor to locate the corresponding entry in the open file table and updates the associated file offset.

dup() system call:

The dup() system call is used to duplicate an existing file descriptor. This can be useful in cases where a process needs to use multiple file descriptors to refer to the same file or device. When a process calls dup() with an existing file descriptor, the kernel creates a new file descriptor that refers to the same open file or device as the original file descriptor.

In the open file table, the new file descriptor is associated with the same entry as the original file descriptor, and both file descriptors share the same file offset and other metadata for the file.

dup2() system call:

The dup2() system call is similar to the dup() system call, but it allows a process to specify the new file descriptor number to use for the duplicated file descriptor. This can be useful in cases where the process needs to use a specific file descriptor number, rather than letting the kernel assign a new one automatically.

When a process opens a new file or device using the open() system call, the kernel assigns a file descriptor to it. The kernel chooses this file descriptor by finding the smallest available non-negative integer that is not currently in use as a file descriptor by the process. The kernel searches through the process's file descriptor table, which is an array of file descriptors associated with the process, to find an available file descriptor.

Typically, the first three file descriptors, 0, 1, and 2, are already in use by convention. File descriptor 0 is the standard input (stdin), file descriptor 1 is the standard output (stdout), and file descriptor 2 is the standard error (stderr). These file descriptors are already open when a process starts.

After the kernel finds an available file descriptor, it creates a new entry in the process's file descriptor table and associates it with the open file or device. The new file descriptor number is then returned to the process by the open() system call.

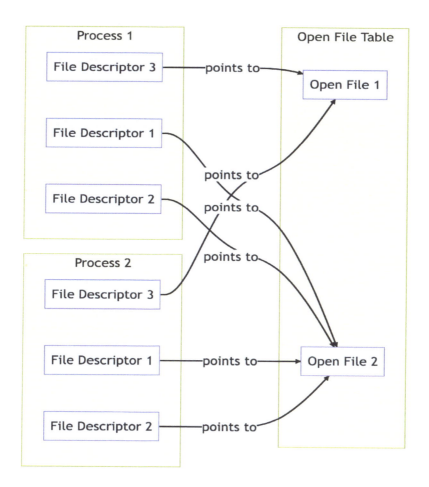

In this visualization, we have two processes: Process 1 and Process 2. Each process has its own file descriptor table with three file descriptors: FD1, FD2, and FD3 for Process 1, and FD1, FD2, and FD3 for Process 2.

There is also an open file table represented by Open File Table, which contains two open files: Open File 1 and Open File 2.

The arrows represent the relationship between the file descriptors and the open files. FD1 and FD2 from both Process 1 and Process 2 point to Open File 2, indicating that they share the same open file. FD3 from both processes point to Open File 1, indicating that they refer to the same open file as well.

Pipes

We will now discuss the concept of Pipes in Linux, and see how it ties together many of the concepts we've been discussing (processes, system calls, IO, file descriptors).

In Linux, pipes are a form of inter-process communication (IPC) that allows data to be exchanged between two processes. A pipe creates a unidirectional communication channel where one process writes data to the pipe, and another process reads that data from the pipe.

Here's how pipes work in Linux:

1. Creating a Pipe

The `pipe()` system call is used to create a pipe. It takes an array of two integers as an argument, typically referred to as `pipefd`. After the `pipe()` call, `pipefd[0]` refers to the read end of the pipe, and `pipefd[1]` refers to the write end of the pipe.

```c
#include <unistd.h>

int pipe(int pipefd[2]);
```

2. IPC Between Two Processes

The pipe allows communication between two related processes, typically created by forking a parent process. When a process forks, it creates an exact copy of itself, including the file descriptors. The parent process can then close one end of the pipe (e.g., the read end) and use the other end (e.g., the write end) to send data to the child process. The child process, in turn, can close the write end and use the read end to receive data from the parent process.

3. Shell Process Creation

In the context of shell commands, when you use the pipe symbol ` | `, the shell creates two processes and sets up a pipe between them. It takes the output of the first command (process) and feeds it as input to the second command (process).

For example:
```bash
ls | grep .txt
```

Here, the shell will create two processes: one for ls and another for grep. The output of ls is sent to the input of grep through a pipe.

4. File Descriptors for Reading/Writing

File descriptors are used to interact with the pipe. When a process writes data to the pipe, it writes to the file descriptor representing the write end of the pipe (pipefd[1]). When a process wants to read data from the pipe, it reads from the file descriptor representing the read end of the pipe (pipefd[0]).

5. System Calls for Reading/Writing

To write data to the pipe, a process uses the `write()` system call, which writes data from a buffer to the file descriptor.

For example:

```c
#include <unistd.h>

ssize_t write(int fd, const void *buf, size_t count);
```

To read data from the pipe, a process uses the `read()` system call, which reads data from a file descriptor into a buffer.

For example:

```c
#include <unistd.h>

ssize_t read(int fd, void *buf, size_t count);
```

By using these system calls, the two processes can communicate with each other through the pipe.

Questions

1. What is a file descriptor in Linux?
2. How are file descriptors used in Linux?
3. What is the maximum number of file descriptors a process can have in Linux?
4. What is the open file table in Linux?
5. What information does the open file table contain?
6. How is the open file table different from a process's file descriptor table?
7. How does a process open a file in Linux?
8. How does the kernel choose a file descriptor number for a newly opened file descriptor?
9. What happens when a process reads from or writes to a file using a shared file descriptor?
10. What happens when a process closes a file descriptor?
11. How can a process share a file descriptor with another process in Linux?
12. Can multiple processes share the same file descriptor in Linux?
13. What happens when two processes share a file descriptor in Linux?
14. How does the kernel handle concurrent access to a shared file descriptor?
15. How does the dup() system call work in Linux?
16. How does the dup2() system call work in Linux?

Chapter 9: Linux File System Implementation

Overview

A Linux file system is a method of organizing and storing files on a computer's storage devices, such as hard drives or solid-state drives. It provides a hierarchical structure for organizing files and directories, along with mechanisms for file access, permissions, and metadata storage.

The Virtual File System (VFS) is an abstraction layer in the Linux kernel that provides a unified interface for different file systems. It allows applications and system components to access files and directories, while abstracting away from the underlying file system implementation. The VFS also provides a set of generic operations that file systems must implement to enable compatibility and interoperability.

File systems are implemented through a combination of software and data structures. The implementation typically involves designing data structures to represent files, directories, metadata, and file system operations. These data structures are managed by software routines that handle file system operations, such as creating, reading, writing, and deleting files.

Ext2

One implementation of a Linux file system is the ext2 (second extended file system). The ext2 file system was widely used in earlier versions of Linux and consists of several components, including:

Superblock: Contains metadata about the file system, such as its size, block size, and the location of other important structures.

Inode table: Stores metadata about individual files, such as permissions, timestamps, and file size. Each file in the ext2 file system has an associated inode entry.

Data blocks: These are used to store the actual file contents. Data blocks are organized into block groups to improve performance and manage fragmentation.

Directory structure: Directories are special files that store references to other files and directories. They use a hierarchical structure, with each directory entry containing the filename and the corresponding inode number.

When a file system operation is performed on ext2, the VFS layer receives the request and forwards it to the appropriate ext2 file system driver. The driver then interacts with the ext2-specific data structures to execute the operation. For example, creating a file involves allocating a new inode entry and data blocks, and updating the directory structure and the superblock to reflect the changes.

Ext2 Data Blocks

In the ext2 file system, data blocks are used to store the actual contents of files. To efficiently manage the storage of file data, it employs a combination of direct, indirect, and doubly indirect pointers.

Direct Pointers: The first twelve entries in the inode structure of ext2 are direct pointers. Each one of these points to a specific data block that contains a portion of the file's content, providing fast access to the most frequently accessed blocks of the file.

Indirect Pointers: The thirteenth entry in the inode structure is a single indirect pointer. This pointer, called the "indirect block," points to a block called the "indirect block table." The indirect block table is an array of pointers, where each pointer points to a data block containing additional file content.

By using the indirect block table, ext2 can extend the file's storage beyond the direct pointers. Each entry in this table points to a data block, effectively adding more blocks to store the file's content.

Doubly Indirect Pointers: The fourteenth entry in the inode structure is a doubly indirect pointer. This pointer, called the "doubly indirect block," points to a block called the "doubly indirect block table." The doubly indirect block table is an array of pointers, where each pointer points to an indirect block table.

By using the doubly indirect block table, ext2 can further extend the file's storage. Each entry in the doubly indirect block table points to an indirect block table, which in turn points to data blocks containing file content. This allows for additional levels of indirection, enabling the storage of a larger amount of file data.

By using a combination of direct, indirect, and doubly indirect pointers, the ext2 file system efficiently allocates and accesses data blocks for storing the contents of files. The direct pointers provide fast access to the initial blocks, while the indirect and doubly indirect pointers allow for dynamic allocation of additional blocks as the file size increases. This flexible storage allocation scheme helps optimize the use of disk space while accommodating files of varying sizes.

Inode Table

In a Linux file system, an inode (short for "index node") is a data structure that stores metadata about a file or directory, such as its permissions, owner, modification time, and the location of the file's data blocks on the disk.

The inode table is a table that contains a list of inodes for all the files and directories in the file system. This table is usually stored in a fixed location on the disk and is typically divided into multiple blocks or sections, each of which contains a certain number of inodes.

Each inode in the table has a unique number that identifies it within the file system. When a new file or directory is created, a new inode is allocated for it, and the inode's metadata is filled in with the appropriate information, such as the file's owner, group, permissions, and size.

In addition to storing metadata, the inode also contains pointers to the data blocks that hold the file's actual content. For small files, the inode may store the data directly within the inode itself, using what are called "direct pointers." For larger files, however, the inode will store pointers to data blocks located elsewhere on the disk.

The inode table also keeps track of which inodes are currently in use and which are free. When a file or directory is deleted, its inode is marked as free, and its corresponding data blocks are released for use by other files or directories.

Directories and File Resolution

When a process wants to access a file or directory in a Linux file system, it typically starts by specifying the file's path, such as /home/user/Documents/file.txt. The path is essentially a sequence of directory names and file names, separated by slashes, that indicates the location of the file or directory within the file system's directory hierarchy.

To access the file's data, the process needs to first locate its corresponding inode in the inode table. This is done by traversing the directory hierarchy from the root directory down to the directory that contains the file, using a series of inode numbers stored in each directory's data blocks. Specifically, when the process specifies a path like /home/user/Documents/file.txt, the file system looks up the inode for the root directory, then follows the inode for the home directory, then the user directory, then the Documents directory, and finally the inode for file.txt.

Each directory contains a list of directory entries that map filenames to their corresponding inode numbers. When the file system needs to locate a file within a directory, it searches through the directory's data blocks to find the corresponding directory entry and retrieves the inode number from that entry.

Once the file's inode has been located, the file system can use the inode's metadata to retrieve the file's data blocks from the disk and provide them to the process for reading or writing. If the file is a directory, the inode will also contain a list of directory entries, allowing the file system to recursively resolve paths within the directory hierarchy.

Hard and Soft Links

In a Linux file system, a hard link is a reference to a file or directory that shares the same underlying inode as the original file or directory. This means that a hard link points directly to the inode of the original file, and any changes made to the original file are immediately visible through the hard link.

When you create a hard link using the ln command, you essentially create a new directory entry that points to the same inode as the original file. Both the original file and the hard link have the same file permissions, ownership, and other metadata since they share the same inode.

Hard links are beneficial because they allow you to create multiple names for the same file or directory without creating additional copies of the data on disk. This can save disk space and reduce the time needed to create or copy files since only a new directory entry needs to be created to create a hard link.

However, hard links have some limitations. For example, they cannot be created for directories that reside on different file systems and can cause confusion if multiple hard links with different names are created for the same file.

In contrast to hard links, which point directly to the inode of the original file, soft links (also known as symbolic links or symlinks) are special files that point to the file name or path of the original file.

When you create a soft link using the `ln -s` command, you create a new file that contains the name or path of the original file. When a process accesses the soft link, the file system looks up the target file or directory based on the path stored in the soft link and provides the data to the process.

Soft links are beneficial because they allow you to create multiple names for the same file or directory, even if they reside on different file systems or partitions. Soft links can also be used to create shortcuts or aliases to files or directories that are buried deep in the file system hierarchy.

However, soft links have some limitations. For example, if the original file or directory is moved or renamed, the soft link may break since it points to the original file or directory by name. Soft links can also cause confusion if multiple soft links with different names are created for the same file or directory since they may appear to be separate files or directories to the user.

Inode Table in Action

When you run the `ls -l` command in a Linux terminal, it lists the contents of a directory and displays detailed information about each file and subdirectory, such as the file permissions, owner, group, size, and modification time.

To obtain this information, `ls -l` reads the directory's inode table, which contains a list of inodes for all the files and directories in the directory. For each inode, `ls -l` reads the associated metadata, such as the file permissions, owner, group, size, and modification time, and displays it in a formatted way.

The information displayed by `ls -l` is typically presented in a series of columns, with each column corresponding to a specific piece of metadata. For example, the first column shows the file permissions, the second column shows the number of hard links to the file, the third column shows the file owner, and so on.

In addition to the metadata displayed by `ls -l`, this command also provides information about the file type, such as whether the file is a regular file, a directory, a symbolic link, or a device file. This information is obtained by examining the file's inode and determining its type based on the inode's file mode.

`ls -l` is a powerful command that relies on the file system's inode table for obtaining detailed information about the files and directories in a Linux file system.

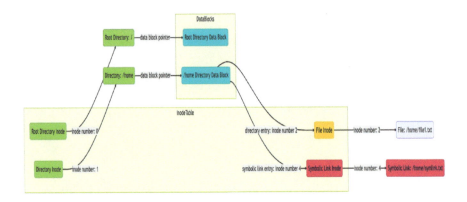

The diagram represents a simplified file system using the ext2 file system as an example. It illustrates the relationships between different components of the file system, including inodes and data blocks.

The diagram consists of two subgraphs: "InodeTable" and "DataBlocks."

The "InodeTable" subgraph contains four inodes:

- "inode number: 0" represents the root directory inode associated with the root directory /.

- "inode number: 1" represents a directory inode, specifically the /home directory.
- "inode number: 2" represents a file inode, specifically the file /home/file1.txt.
- "inode number: 4" represents a symbolic link inode, specifically the symbolic link /home/symlink.txt.

The "DataBlocks" diagram block contains three data blocks:

- rootDataBlock represents the data block associated with the root directory /.
- homeDataBlock represents the data block associated with the /home directory.
- fileDataBlock represents the data block associated with the file /home/file1.txt and the symbolic link /home/symlink.txt.

The connections between the inodes and data blocks illustrate the relationships:

- The root directory inode inode0 points to the root directory data block rootDataBlock.
- The /home directory inode inode1 points to the /home directory data block homeDataBlock.
- The /home directory data block homeDataBlock contains a directory entry that references the file inode inode2, representing the file /home/file1.txt.
- The /home directory data block homeDataBlock also contains a symbolic link entry that references the symbolic link inode inode4, representing the symbolic link /home/symlink.txt.

Questions

1. What is a file system?
2. What is an inode table?
3. What is a direct pointer?
4. What is an indirect pointer?
5. What is a doubly indirect pointer?
6. What is a directory?
7. What is a file?
8. What is a hard link?
9. What is a symbolic link?
10. What is the difference between a hard link and a symbolic link?
11. What is a block?
12. What is a superblock?
13. What is a file descriptor?
14. What is a file system driver?
15. What is a file system mount point?
16. What is a file system journal?

Chapter 10: Sockets

Overview

Sockets in the Linux kernel are a fundamental mechanism for network communication. They provide an interface for processes to send and receive data over the network, facilitating communication between different machines or processes running on the same machine. Here's an overview of sockets in the Linux kernel:

Socket API: The Linux kernel exposes a socket API that allows user-space applications to create, configure, and interact with sockets by providing a set of system calls that applications can use to perform various socket operations, such as socket creation, binding, listening, connecting, sending, and receiving data.

Socket Data Structures: In the Linux kernel, sockets are represented by data structures. The main data structure is "struct socket", which contains information about the socket's type, state, protocol, file operations, and other attributes. Each socket is associated with a file descriptor that user-space processes can use to access the socket.

Socket Types: The Linux kernel supports different socket types, such as TCP/IP sockets, UDP sockets, raw sockets, Unix domain sockets. Each socket type has its own characteristics and usage patterns. For example, TCP/IP sockets provide reliable, connection-oriented communication, while UDP sockets offer unreliable, connectionless communication.

Protocol Handlers: The Linux kernel implements various protocol handlers to handle different socket types and protocols. These handlers, often implemented as kernel modules, provide the necessary functionality to process and manage socket-specific operations. For instance, the TCP protocol handler handles TCP/IP sockets, while the UDP protocol handler handles UDP sockets.

Network Stack: Sockets are an integral part of the Linux networking stack. The networking stack is responsible for managing network connections, routing, packet transmission, and other networking tasks. Sockets interact with the networking stack to send and receive data packets, perform protocol-specific operations, and handle network-related events.

Socket Buffer: When data is sent or received through a socket, it is stored in a socket buffer, which is a kernel data structure that holds the data until it is processed. The socket buffer is managed by the kernel and is associated with each socket. Socket buffers are used to handle data transmission, buffering, and flow control within the kernel.

Socket Options: Sockets in the Linux kernel support various socket options that allow applications to configure the socket behavior. Socket options can control features such as socket timeout, buffer sizes, socket-level multicast settings, and more. These are typically set using the `setsockopt()` system call.

Overall, sockets in the Linux kernel provide a powerful and flexible mechanism for network communication. They allow processes to establish connections, exchange data, and interact with the underlying networking infrastructure, enabling a wide range of networking applications and protocols.

System Calls

To interact with sockets in Linux, various system calls are provided, such as:

`socket()` - Creates a new socket and returns a file descriptor that can be used to access the socket.

`bind()` - Associates a socket with a specific address, such as an IP address and port number.

`listen()` - Prepares a socket to accept incoming connections.

`accept()` - Waits for a connection request to arrive and returns a new socket for communicating with the client.

`connect()` - Establishes a connection to a remote socket.

`send()` - Sends data over a socket.

`recv()` - Receives data from a socket.

`close()` - Closes a socket and releases its resources.

These system calls can be used by applications to create, configure, and communicate over sockets in Linux.

Unix Domain Sockets

Unix domain sockets are a type of socket available in Unix-like operating systems, including Linux, that provide a mechanism for IPC between processes on the same machine. Unix domain sockets use a file system path as an address rather than an IP address and port number like network sockets.

One common use case for Unix domain sockets is in client-server applications running on the same machine. For example, a web server running on a Linux machine might use a Unix domain socket to communicate with a backend application that is also running on the same machine.

Another use case for Unix domain sockets is in container environments, where processes running inside a container may need to communicate with processes running on the host system.

Here's an example of how Unix domain sockets can be used in a simple client-server application:

- The server creates a Unix domain socket using the `socket()` system call and binds it to a file system path using the `bind()` system call.

- The server listens for incoming connections on the socket using the `listen()` system call.

- The client connects to the server by creating a Unix domain socket using the `socket()` system call and connecting to the server's file system path using the `connect()` system call.

- Once the connection is established, the client and server can communicate over the socket using the `send()` and `recv()` system calls.

Questions

1. What is a socket?
2. What types of sockets are available in Linux?
3. What is the difference between a TCP/IP socket and a UDP socket?
4. What is a Unix domain socket?
5. How do you create a Unix domain socket?
6. How do you bind a Unix domain socket to a file system path?
7. How do you listen for incoming connections on a Unix domain socket?
8. How do you accept incoming connections on a Unix domain socket?
9. How do you connect to a Unix domain socket from a client process?

Chapter 11: Boot Process

Overview

The boot process of a Linux system involves several steps, which can vary depending on the specific distribution and configuration. Here's a generalized diagram of the Linux boot process:

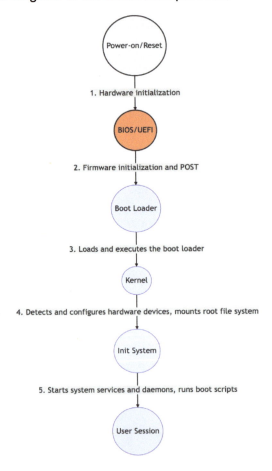

Here's a brief explanation of each step:

- **Power-on or Reset**: The computer is turned on or restarted, and the basic hardware initialization begins.
- **BIOS/UEFI**: The Basic Input/Output System (BIOS) or Unified Extensible Firmware Interface (UEFI) firmware initializes and performs a Power-On Self-Test (POST) to check the hardware components.
- **Boot Loader**: The boot loader (such as GRUB or LILO) is loaded and executed from the boot sector of the hard disk or some other bootable device. It presents a menu of available kernels and options, then loads the selected kernel into memory.
- **Kernel**: The Linux kernel is loaded into memory and initialized. It detects and configures the hardware devices, mounts the root file system, and starts the init process.
- **Init System**: The init system (such as systemd or SysVinit) is responsible for starting and stopping system services and daemons, and running scripts during the boot process. It also sets up the user environment and launches the user session.
- **User Session**: The user session starts, typically with a login screen or graphical desktop environment, and the user can begin using the system.

Questions

1. What is the role of the BIOS/UEFI in the boot process?
2. What is a boot loader?
3. What is the function of the Linux kernel during boot?
4. What is the root file system?
5. What is an init system?
6. What is the difference between systemd and SysVinit?
7. What is a user session?
8. What happens if the kernel fails to boot?
9. Can the boot process be customized?

Chapter 12: Troubleshooting

In addition to the theoretical evaluation of Linux internals, the Linux Systems interview might also contain questions about troubleshooting system issues. These troubleshooting questions are generally of the form: you are faced with the following symptom, explain how you would approach this problem and find the root cause.

Interviewers often are Linux experts, or at least experts at the question they give you, so they can dive very deep. They generally try to push you as far as you can go. They will give you clues or hints about what certain command outputs would be so that you can continue troubleshooting.

For this chapter, we'll start with fundamental system resources that are most often analyzed, cover some general Linux tools that can analyze these resources, and finally go through some scenarios that illustrate how you can use what we've learned to diagnose an issue.

Fundamental Analysis

After reading some of the core theoretical topics of the Linux kernel relevant to these interviews, you should have a decent understanding of what makes up the Linux system and the mechanics of its internals. At a fundamental level, the OS is providing system abstractions. The process is an abstraction of a running program. Hardware resources are then abstracted to the user programs (processes) to make it easier for them to interact with the hardware.

The core hardware resources are CPU, Memory, Disk I/O and Network I/O.

These are, therefore, the terms in which most system-issue diagnoses will be performed. Once we get a symptom (e.g., a ticket for high disk or inode usage or CPU reaching 100%), we start with analyzing the corresponding hardware resource. Most times, there is a process or group of processes that are causing issues with the hardware resources. Therefore, we trace backward from the constrained/impacted hardware resources toward the process causing the issue.

Common Tools

There's a plethora of Linux tools to analyze each of these resources. We will just look at the basic tools that should be available on all systems. The idea here is not to be prescriptive on the exact commands and options to run but to understand the intent for each step of the troubleshooting process and find *some* tool you can use to acquire the relevant information.

General Process and Memory Tools

ps

The `ps auxww` command is used to display a detailed list of all running processes on a Linux system. Let's break down the options and provide an example output:

```
Options:

a: Shows processes from all users, rather than just
the current user.
u: Displays a detailed format listing, including the
user, CPU usage, memory usage, start time, and more.
x: Includes processes that have no controlling
terminal (e.g., daemons).
ww: Prevents the output from being truncated and
ensures that the full command-line arguments are
displayed.
```

```
USER         PID %CPU %MEM    VSZ   RSS TTY        STAT
START   TIME COMMAND
root           1  0.0  0.2 169828  9428 ?          Ss
Mar24   0:14 /sbin/init
root           2  0.0  0.0      0     0 ?          S
Mar24   0:00 [kthreadd]
root           3  0.0  0.0      0     0 ?          I<
Mar24   0:00 [rcu_gp]
root           4  0.0  0.0      0     0 ?          I<
Mar24   0:00 [rcu_par_gp]
```

```
USER: The username of the process owner.
PID: The process ID of the running process.
%CPU: The CPU usage of the process.
%MEM: The memory usage of the process.
VSZ: The virtual memory size of the process.
RSS: The resident set size (actual memory usage) of
the process.
TTY: The controlling terminal associated with the
process.
STAT: The process state (e.g., S for sleeping, R for
running, Z for zombie).
START: The start time or date of the process.
TIME: The total CPU time consumed by the process.
COMMAND: The command-line used to launch the process.
```

top

The top command is used to monitor system processes and their resource utilization in real-time. It provides a dynamic, interactive view of the processes running on a Linux system.

```
Common Options:

-c: Displays the command-line arguments of processes.
-n <num>: Specifies the number of iterations/top
output refreshes.
-p <pid(s)>: Monitors specific process IDs.
-u <username>: Shows processes owned by a specific
user.
-k: Displays memory values in kilobytes instead of
the default (bytes).
1: Displays per-CPU statistics.
```

d <delay>: Specifies the delay between updates in seconds.
q: Quits top without delay.

Example output:

```
top - 11:35:17 up 5 days,  3:27,  1 user,  load
average: 0.45, 0.65, 0.70
Tasks: 217 total,   2 running, 215 sleeping,   0
stopped,   0 zombie
%Cpu(s):  2.8 us,  1.5 sy,  0.0 ni, 95.4 id,  0.2 wa,
0.0 hi,  0.0 si,  0.1 st
MiB Mem :  15930.2 total,   3317.2 free,   8405.2
used,   4212.8 buff/cache
MiB Swap:  2048.0 total,   2048.0 free,      0.0
used.   6563.4 avail Mem

   PID USER       PR  NI    VIRT    RES    SHR S  %CPU
%MEM     TIME+ COMMAND
  1665 john       20   0 2030936 117732  58172 S   2.3
0.7   2:43.34 gnome-shell
  2295 john       20   0 2134100 237832  81276 S   1.7
1.5   1:39.29 firefox
  1259 root       20   0  809004  93200  64164 S   0.3
0.6   0:18.97 Xorg
```

The top line displays the current time, system uptime, the number of logged-in users, and the load average.

The second line shows the number of tasks/processes categorized by their status (running, sleeping, stopped, and zombie).

%Cpu(s) provides CPU utilization statistics, including user, system, nice (low priority), idle, wait, and hardware interrupt time.

MiB Mem displays memory information, including total, free, used, and buffer/cache memory.

MiB Swap shows swap space information, including total, free, and used swap memory.

The process list below provides details about individual processes, including their process ID (PID), user, priority (PR), virtual memory (VIRT), resident memory (RES), shared memory (SHR), CPU usage (%CPU), memory usage (%MEM), and cumulative CPU time (TIME+).

free

The `free` command displays information about the system's total, used, and available memory.

Common options:

```
-h or --human-readable: Prints sizes in human-
readable format.
```

Example output:

```
              total          used          free
shared   buff/cache     available
Mem:            3.7Gi         1.5Gi         562Mi
282Mi         1.6Gi         1.5Gi
Swap:             0B            0B            0B
```

top

The command `top` provides a dynamic real-time view of the system, including the memory usage of a processes.

Common options:

```
Shift + M: Sorts the processes based on their memory
usage.
```

Example output:

```
top - 12:34:56 up 1 day,  2:15,  1 user,  load
average: 0.00, 0.00, 0.00
Tasks: 209 total,  1 running, 208 sleeping,  0
stopped,  0 zombie
```

```
%Cpu(s):  0.0 us,  0.0 sy,  0.0 ni,100.0 id,  0.0 wa,
0.0 hi,  0.0 si,  0.0 st
MiB Mem :   3889.6 total,    434.8 free,    1644.9
used,    1809.9 buff/cache
MiB Swap:      0.0 total,      0.0 free,       0.0
used.   2079.7 avail Mem

  PID USER       PR  NI    VIRT    RES    SHR S  %CPU
%MEM      TIME+ COMMAND
 1234 username  20   0 3232324 548156  12356 S   0.0
8.1   0:10.25 process1
 5678 username  20   0 1055764 123456   9876 S   0.0
3.2   0:05.80 process2
```

vmstat

The vmstat command is a useful tool for monitoring virtual memory statistics on Linux systems. It provides information about processes, memory, paging, block I/O, CPU usage, and more. Here are some common options and an example output:

Common options:

```
-a or --active: Displays active/inactive memory
statistics.
-s or --stats: Displays a summary of virtual memory
statistics.
-S <unit>: Specifies the unit for memory sizes (e.g.,
k for kilobytes, m for megabytes).
```

Example output:

```
procs  -----------memory---------- ---swap-- -----io-
--- -system-- ------cpu-----
  r  b   swpd   free   buff  cache   si   so    bi
 bo   in   cs  us  sy  id  wa
```

```
 1   0        0 258452  65472 456760     0     0        1
 12   45   91   5   3  92   0
```

Explanation of the output:

```
procs: Number of processes waiting for run time or
blocked.
r: The number of processes in the running state.
b: The number of processes in uninterruptible sleep.
swpd: Amount of virtual memory used (in kilobytes).
free: Amount of idle memory (in kilobytes).
buff: Memory used as buffers (in kilobytes).
cache: Memory used as cache (in kilobytes).
si: Amount of memory swapped in from disk (in
kilobytes per second).
so: Amount of memory swapped to disk (in kilobytes
per second).
bi: Blocks received from a block device (in blocks
per second).
bo: Blocks sent to a block device (in blocks per
second).
in: Interrupts per second, including the clock.
cs: Context switches per second.
us: Percentage of CPU time spent in user space.
sy: Percentage of CPU time spent in kernel space.
id: Percentage of idle CPU time.
wa: Percentage of CPU time spent waiting for I/O.
```

Disk/IO Tools

To analyze disk I/O utilization and errors on a Linux system, you can use several commands:

iostat

Reports CPU utilization and I/O statistics for disks and partitions.

Common options:

```
-x: Provides extended disk statistics, including
utilization percentages.
-d <interval> <count>: Sets the sampling interval and
the number of reports to generate.
```

Example output:

```
Linux 5.4.0-74-generic (hostname)   06/04/23
_x86_64_   (4 CPU)

Device              tps   kB_read/s   kB_wrtn/s
kB_dscd/s     kB_read   kB_wrtn   kB_dscd
sda             .  1.07          0.63        14.14
0.00          2K        60K           0
sdb                0.01          0.02         0.02
0.00          60B       60B           0
```

Explanation of output:

```
Device: Disk or partition name.
tps: Number of transfers per second.
kB_read/s: Kilobytes read per second.
kB_wrtn/s: Kilobytes written per second.
kB_dscd/s: Kilobytes discarded per second.
kB_read: Total kilobytes read.
kB_wrtn: Total kilobytes written.
kB_dscd: Total kilobytes discarded.
```

iotop

Monitors and displays real-time I/O usage information for processes.

Common options:

```
-o: Only shows processes that perform I/O.
-d <interval>: Sets the delay between updates.
```

Example output:

```
Total DISK READ:        0.00 B/s | Total DISK WRITE:
0.00 B/s
Current DISK READ:      0.00 B/s | Current DISK WRITE:
0.00 B/s
TID  PRIO  USER        DISK READ  DISK WRITE  SWAPIN
IO    COMMAND
   1 be/4 root           0.00 B/s     0.00 B/s  0.00 %
0.00 % systemd --switched-root --system --deserialize
23
   2 be/4 root           0.00 B/s     0.00 B/s  0.00 %
```

```
0.00 % [kthreadd]
```

dmesg

Displays the system message buffer, including disk-related error messages.

Common options:

```
-T: Show timestamps.
```

Example output:

```
[Thu Jun  4 12:34:56 2023] sd 0:0:0:0: [sda] Sense
Key : Medium Error [current] [descriptor]
[Thu Jun  4 12:34:56 2023] sd 0:0:0:0: [sda] Add.
Sense: Unrecovered read error - auto reallocate
failed
```

Networking Tools

ss

The `ss` command is another useful tool for analyzing network connections and socket statistics on a Linux system. It provides more detailed information compared to the `netstat` command. Here are some common options and an example output:

Common options:

```
-t: Displays TCP sockets.
-u: Displays UDP sockets.
-n: Shows numerical addresses instead of resolving
```

them.
```
-p: Shows the process using the socket.
-s: Displays socket statistics summary.
```

Example output:

```
State          Recv-Q       Send-Q                 Local
Address:Port            Peer Address:Port
ESTAB          0            0
192.168.1.100:22              192.168.1.200:12345
TIME-WAIT      0            0
192.168.1.100:8080            192.168.1.201:56789
```

Explanation of output:

```
State: The state of the socket connection (e.g.,
ESTABLISHED, TIME-WAIT).
Recv-Q: The number of bytes in the receive queue.
Send-Q: The number of bytes in the send queue.
Local Address:Port: The local IP address and port
number.
Peer Address:Port: The remote IP address and port
number.
```

Note: The above example output only shows a few sample entries. The actual `ss` output can include more connections and socket information.

The `ss -n DEV` command is used to display network interface statistics. It provides detailed information about network interfaces, including the number of packets transmitted and received, errors, and drops.

Here's an example output:

```
State      Recv-Q    Send-Q              Local
Address:Port    Peer Address:Port
ESTAB      0         0                   192.168.1.100:22
192.168.1.200:12345
TIME-WAIT 0         0
192.168.1.100:8080    192.168.1.201:56789

Netid              State              Recv-Q
Send-Q                    Local Address:Port    Peer
Address:Port
nlpid              UNCONN             0
0
nlpid              UNCONN             0
0
```

Explanation of output:

The first part of the output is the same as the example output provided earlier, showing socket information.

The second part provides network interface statistics, including the netid, state, receive queue (Recv-Q), send queue (Send-Q), local address and port, and peer address and port.

sar

For network troubleshooting, the `sar -n DEV` command can be used to display network statistics and performance metrics. It provides valuable information about network devices and their utilization.

Here's an example command and its output:

Command:

```
sar -n DEV
```

Example output:

```
Linux 5.4.0-70-generic (hostname)     06/01/23
_x86_64_     (4 CPU)

09:00:01 AM     IFACE   rxpck/s   txpck/s    rxkB/s
txkB/s    rxcmp/s   txcmp/s   rxmcst/s   %ifutil
09:10:01 AM             eth0    355.40    456.50     65.63
102.10      0.00      0.00      0.00      0.00
09:10:01 AM             lo       55.40     25.50     34.63
5.10       0.00      0.00      0.00      0.00
```

Explanation of output:

```
IFACE: The network interface name.
rxpck/s: Number of packets received per second.
txpck/s: Number of packets transmitted per second.
rxkB/s: Kilobytes received per second.
```

txkB/s: Kilobytes transmitted per second.
rxcmp/s: Compressed packets received per second.
txcmp/s: Compressed packets transmitted per second.
rxmcst/s: Multicast packets received per second.
%ifutil: Network **interface** utilization percentage.

netstat

Displays network connection information, routing tables, and network interface statistics.

Common options:

-i: Displays network **interface** statistics.

Example output:

```
Kernel Interface table
Iface    MTU Met    RX-OK RX-ERR RX-DRP RX-OVR    TX-OK
TX-ERR TX-DRP TX-OVR Flg
eth0    1500   0      2890      0      0      0
1562      0      0      0 BMRU
lo    65536   0         0      0      0      0
0      0      0      0 LRU
```

Explanation of output:

RX-OK: Packets received without errors.
RX-ERR: Receive errors.
RX-DRP: Dropped packets due to buffer overflow or other reasons.
RX-OVR: Receive overruns (when the receiver cannot process packets quickly enough).
TX-OK: Packets transmitted without errors.
TX-ERR: Transmit errors.
TX-DRP: Dropped packets during transmission.
TX-OVR: Transmit overruns (when the sender cannot

provide packets quickly enough).

Additional Deep Diving Tools

strace

The strace command is a powerful tool for debugging and analyzing system calls made by a process. It can help identify issues, track system interactions, and gather information about the behavior of a program. Here are some common examples of using strace along with example outputs:

Basic usage: Running a command with strace to trace its system calls.

Command:

```
strace ls
```

Example output:

```
execve("/bin/ls", ["ls"], 0x7fff56eb6338 /* 36 vars
*/) = 0
brk(NULL)                               =
0x5610d256f000
arch_prctl(0x3001 /* ARCH_??? */, 0x7fff56eb5a60) = -
1 EINVAL (Invalid argument)
access("/etc/ld.so.preload", R_OK)      = -1 ENOENT
(No such file or directory)
openat(AT_FDCWD, "/etc/ld.so.cache",
O_RDONLY|O_CLOEXEC) = 3
```

Explanation:

```
execve: Shows the execution of the ls command.
brk: Indicates a request for a new heap memory space.
arch_prctl: Performs architecture-specific control
operations.
access: Checks the access permissions for a file.
openat: Opens a file or directory.
```

Tracing a specific process by its PID: Tracing a running process by specifying its PID.

Command:

```
strace -p <PID>
```

Example output:

```
Process 12345 attached
futex(0x7fe19bd7c838, FUTEX_WAKE_PRIVATE, 2147483647)
= 0
read(4, "Hello, world!\n", 4096)          = 14
```

Explanation:

```
futex: Performs operations on futexes, which are fast
user-space mutexes.
read: Reads data from a file descriptor.
```

Filtering system calls: Specifying which system calls to trace using the -e option.

Command:

```
strace -e open,close ls
```

Example output:

```
openat(AT_FDCWD, ".",
O_RDONLY|O_NONBLOCK|O_DIRECTORY|O_CLOEXEC) = 3
close(3)                                  = 0
```

Explanation:

```
Only the open and close system calls are traced for
the ls command.
```

lsof

The lsof (List Open Files) command is used to list open files, network connections, and various types of file-related information on a Linux system. It also provides detailed insights into which files and processes are currently accessing or using specific resources.

<u>Listing all open files: Displaying all open files and associated processes.</u>

Command:

```
lsof
```

Example output:

```
COMMAND     PID  USER   FD    TYPE DEVICE SIZE/OFF
NODE NAME
systemd      1  root   cwd    DIR   8,1     4096
2 /
```

```
systemd        1  root  txt   REG    8,1  1866112
4293927 /usr/lib/systemd/systemd
```

Explanation:

```
COMMAND: The name of the command or process.
PID: The process ID of the command.
USER: The user associated with the process.
FD: The file descriptor used by the process.
TYPE: The type of the file (e.g., REG for regular
file, DIR for directory).
DEVICE: The device number.
SIZE/OFF: The size or offset of the file.
NODE: The inode number of the file.
NAME: The name of the file or file path.
```

Filtering by a specific user: Listing open files for a specific user.

Command:

```
lsof -u <username>
```

Example output:

```
COMMAND     PID  USER    FD    TYPE DEVICE SIZE/OFF
NODE NAME
chrome   12345  user   cwd    DIR    8,1     4096
1234567 /home/user
chrome   12345  user   txt    REG    8,1  1866112
4293927 /usr/bin/chrome
```

Showing network connections: Listing open network connections.

Command:

```
lsof -i
```

Example output:

```
COMMAND  PID   USER   FD    TYPE DEVICE SIZE/OFF NODE
NAME
chrome 12345  user   124u  IPv4  12345      0t0  TCP
localhost:8080->localhost:54321 (ESTABLISHED)
```

Explanation:

```
FD: The file descriptor used for the connection.
TYPE: The type of connection (e.g., IPv4, IPv6).
NODE: The local and remote addresses and ports.
NAME: The state of the connection.
```

Find which process has a specific file open

```
lsof /path/to/file
```

Replace /path/to/file with the actual path and name of the file you want to check. The lsof command will display the processes that have the specified file open, along with other relevant information.

Example output:

```
COMMAND     PID   USER   FD    TYPE DEVICE SIZE/OFF
NODE NAME
firefox    1234  user   txt   REG   8,17  1234567
123456 /path/to/file
```

Explanation:

```
COMMAND: The name of the command or process.
PID: The process ID of the command.
USER: The user associated with the process.
FD: The file descriptor used by the process.
TYPE: The type of the file.
DEVICE: The device number.
SIZE/OFF: The size or offset of the file.
NODE: The inode number of the file.
NAME: The name of the file.
```

Scenarios

Now that we've covered some tools that can be used to diagnose system issues, let's look at some example system troubleshooting interview questions and how they can be answered:

Question: You get a ticket that a bad file keeps growing and filling up disk space. How would you approach this?

Possible answer:

Here's a systematic approach to address the issue:

Identify the file: Begin by locating the specific file that is consuming disk space. This can be done using various methods, such as examining disk usage reports (df or du) or using file exploration tools (ls, find, etc.).

Use lsof to identify the process: Once you have identified the file, you can use the lsof command with the file name as an argument to determine which process has the file open. Running `lsof` `/path/to/file` will provide information about the process associated with the file, including its PID.

Perform strace on the process: Utilize the `strace` command with the PID from the previous step to trace the system calls made by the process. Running `strace -p <PID>` attaches `strace` to the process and displays detailed information about its activities, including file operations.

By examining the `strace` output, you can identify the specific file-related system calls made by the process, such as open, write, or truncate. This can help pinpoint any erroneous behavior or abnormal file operations.

Investigate the application logs: Check the logs of the application associated with the problematic process. Application logs might provide insights into any error messages, warnings, or unusual behavior that could explain the file growth.

Check for configuration issues: Examine the configuration settings of the application or process involved. Misconfigured settings, such as log rotation or backup mechanisms, could contribute to the file's continuous growth.

Consider other system monitoring tools: Utilize additional system monitoring tools like iotop or sysstat to gather information about disk I/O, CPU, and memory usage. These tools can help identify abnormal resource utilization patterns that may contribute to the file growth.

Implement a resolution: Once the root cause has been identified, you can proceed with the appropriate resolution. This might involve fixing the application configuration, modifying the logging settings, addressing code issues, or implementing file size limits.

This is a general troubleshooting approach, and the specific steps may vary depending on the system, file type, and context of the issue at hand.

Question: You are faced with an alarm indicating high p90 API latency coming from a particular host. How would you approach this?

Possible Answer:

Check system resource utilization: Start by checking the overall system resource utilization to identify any bottlenecks. The key areas to investigate include CPU, memory, disk I/O wait time, and network utilization.

- **To check CPU utilization**: Use tools like top, htop, or sar to monitor CPU usage, identify any high CPU load, and determine if it's causing the high latency.
- **To check memory utilization**: Use commands like `free`

or tools like top to analyze memory usage and ensure that memory is not a limiting factor.

- **To check disk I/O wait time**: Utilize tools like iostat or sar to monitor disk I/O performance and identify if high disk I/O wait times are affecting the API latency.
- **To check network utilization**: Tools like ifconfig, sar, or netstat can help analyze network interface statistics to ensure that network congestion is not contributing to the latency issue.

Identify the process causing high CPU user time: If CPU utilization is high, focus on identifying the process responsible for the high CPU user time. This can be achieved through various tools and commands:

- Use tools like top, htop, or ps to identify the processes consuming the most CPU resources.
- Sort the processes based on CPU usage to find the process with the highest CPU utilization.

Investigate the process with high CPU usage:

- **Check the application logs**: Review the application logs related to the identified process to detect any errors, warnings, or anomalies that could explain the high CPU usage.
- **Inspect code and configuration**: Examine the code and configuration of the application to identify any potential inefficiencies, resource leaks, or misconfigurations that could

lead to high CPU utilization.

- **Analyze database queries**: If the process interacts with a database, investigate whether slow or inefficient database queries are contributing to the high CPU usage.

Perform strace on the process: If necessary, use the `strace` command to trace the system calls made by the identified process. This can provide detailed insights into the operations being performed and identify any specific system calls causing high CPU time.

- Run `strace -p <PID>` to attach `strace` to the process and observe its system call activity.
- Analyze the `strace` output to identify any abnormal or repetitive system calls that may indicate inefficient code or other issues.

Consider performance optimizations:

- **Optimize code**: Identify and optimize any inefficient code sections or algorithms that contribute to high CPU usage.
- **Scale horizontally or vertically**: If the application workload is consistently pushing the CPU limits, consider scaling the infrastructure horizontally (adding more servers) or vertically (increasing the CPU capacity) to handle the load.

Answers to Questions

Chapter 1:

1. What is an OS interrupt?

A: An OS interrupt is a signal that the operating system receives from either hardware or software.

2. What is an Interrupt Request (IRQ)?

A: An IRQ is a signal sent by a hardware device to the CPU to request attention from the operating system.

3. What is an Interrupt Handler?

A: An Interrupt Handler is a routine in the OS responsible for servicing an interrupt request.

4. What is an Interrupt Service Routine (ISR)?

A: An ISR is a specific routine designed to handle a particular type of interrupt.

5. What is Interrupt Masking?

A: Interrupt masking is a mechanism that allows the OS to prioritize interrupt requests and prevent them from interfering with critical tasks.

6. What is Interrupt Nesting?

A: Interrupt nesting is a feature that allows multiple interrupts to occur at the same time, with the CPU saving the state of the interrupted process and handling the new interrupt.

7. What is the Interrupt Vector Table (IVT)?

A: The IVT is a data structure in the OS that contains information about each interrupt request.

8. How does an ISR return control back to the Interrupt Handler routine?

A: Once the ISR has completed its task, it returns control back to the Interrupt Handler routine.

9. How do interrupts help the OS manage multiple tasks?

A: Interrupts allow the OS to stop the current process and switch to another process to handle the interrupt request.

10. Why are OS interrupts important?

A: OS interrupts are important because they allow hardware devices and software processes to communicate with the OS and each other, allowing the former to manage multiple tasks and respond quickly to events without wasting CPU resources.

Chapter 2:

1. What are system calls?

A: System calls are the interface between user-level applications and the kernel-level OS. They allow applications to perform various tasks such as reading and writing files, creating processes, managing memory, and communicating with the network.

2. Why are system calls important?

A: System calls are important because they provide a standardized way for applications to interact with the OS. This makes it easier for developers to write portable applications that can run on different OSs.

3. What happens when an application makes a system call?

A: When an application makes a system call, it triggers a software interrupt that transfers control from user mode to kernel mode. The kernel then performs the requested operation and returns control to the application.

4. How are system calls implemented in Linux?

A: In Linux, system calls are implemented as functions in the kernel. These functions are called by applications through a special software interrupt mechanism.

5. What is the purpose of the system call table?

A: The system call table is a data structure in the kernel that maps system call numbers to their corresponding kernel functions. It allows the kernel to efficiently handle system calls made by user-level applications.

6. What is the difference between a system call and a library call?

A: A system call is a request made by an application to the OS while a library call is a request made by an application to a shared library. System calls require a context switch to kernel mode while library calls do not.

7. What is strace?

A: strace is a debugging utility in Linux that allows developers to trace system calls made by an application. It can be used to diagnose problems in applications that interact with the OS.

8. What is ltrace?

A: ltrace is a debugging utility in Linux that allows developers to trace library calls made by an application. It can be used to diagnose problems in applications that rely on shared libraries.

9. What is ftrace?

A: ftrace is a tracing utility in Linux that allows developers to trace various events in the kernel, including system calls, function calls, and interrupts. It can be used for performance analysis and debugging kernel-related issues.

10. What is the difference between strace and ltrace?

A: strace traces system calls made by an application while ltrace traces library calls made by an application. System calls are made to the OS while library calls are made to shared libraries.

11. What is the difference between strace and ftrace?

A: strace operates at the user-level while ftrace operates at the kernel-level. Moreover, strace traces system calls made by an application while ftrace can trace various events in the kernel, including system calls, function calls, and interrupts.

12. What are some common system calls used by all programs?

A: Common system calls used by all programs include open(), close(), read(), write(), fork(), exec(), getpid(), getppid(), mmap(), socket(), connect(), and exit().

13. What is the purpose of the open() system call?

A: The open() system call is used to open files or other resources. It takes a filename and flags as input and returns a file descriptor that can be used for subsequent read() and write() operations.

14. What is the purpose of the fork() system call?

A: The fork() system call is used to create a new process that is a copy of the parent process. It returns the PID of the child process to the parent process and 0 to the child process.

15. What is the purpose of the mmap() system call?

A: The purpose of the mmap() system call is to map files or devices into a process's virtual address space, allowing direct and efficient access to data without the need for explicit read/write system calls. It is used for improved I/O performance, shared memory between processes, and zero-copy techniques.

Chapter 3:

1. What is a zombie process?

A: A zombie process is a process that has completed execution but still has an entry in the process table.

2. How does a process become a zombie?

A: A process becomes a zombie when its parent process fails to call the wait() system call to collect its exit status.

3. How can you find a zombie process?

A: You can find a zombie process by using the ps command with the "aux" option and looking for processes with a "Z" in the STAT column.

4. Can a zombie process consume system memory?

A: The only memory usage is from the process table entry

5. Can a zombie process consume CPU time?

A: No, a zombie process does not consume any CPU time.

6. What is the main problem with zombie processes?

A: If zombie processes are not reaped, they will continue to occupy an entry in the process table, and their PIDs cannot be reused until they are collected by the parent. If a large number of zombie processes accumulate, it can exhaust the available process table entries, leading to errors such as "fork: resource temporarily unavailable" when attempting to create new processes.

7. How can you terminate a zombie process?

A: You can terminate a zombie process by using the "kill" command with the PID.

8. What is an orphan process?

A: An orphan process is a process that is still running but has lost its parent process.

9. How does a process become an orphan?

A: A process becomes an orphan when its parent process terminates before it does.

10. What happens to an orphan process?

A: An orphan process is inherited by the init process (process with ID 1), which becomes its new parent.

11. What system call is used to create a new process in Linux?

A: The fork() system call is used to create a new process in Linux.

12. What is the exec() system call in Linux?

A: The exec() system call is used to replace the current process image with a new process image.

13. How can you get the PID of the current process in Linux?

A: The getpid() system call is used to get the pID of the current process in Linux.

14. What system call is used to wait for a child process to terminate in Linux?

A: The wait() or waitpid() system call is used to wait for a child process to terminate in Linux.

15. What system call is used to change the priority of a process in Linux?

A: The setpriority() system call is used to change the priority of a process in Linux.

16. What system call is used to terminate a process in Linux?

A: The exit() or exit_group() system call is used to terminate a process in Linux.

Chapter 4:

1. What is memory management?

A: Memory management refers to the process of coordinating and controlling computer memory, including the allocation, tracking, and organization of memory resources. It involves managing the usage of physical memory (RAM) and virtual memory to efficiently store and retrieve data for running processes and the OS.

2. Why is memory management important?

A: Memory management is crucial for several reasons:

- It allows multiple processes to share the limited physical memory effectively, enabling multitasking and concurrent execution.

- It enables the OS to provide virtual memory, which allows processes to access more memory than physically available.

- Proper memory management helps prevent issues like memory leaks and out-of-memory errors.

- Efficient memory management contributes to system stability, performance, and overall user experience.

3. What is virtual memory?

A: Virtual memory is a memory management technique that enables processes to access more memory than is physically available in a computer. It creates the illusion of a large, contiguous memory space for each process by using a combination of physical memory (RAM) and disk space.

4. What is a page table?

A: A page table is a data structure used in virtual memory systems to map virtual addresses to physical addresses. It is maintained by the OS for each process and contains entries that associate virtual memory pages with their corresponding physical memory frames.

5. How is the dirty bit used in memory management?

A: The dirty bit, also known as a modify bit, is a flag in a page table entry that indicates whether the corresponding page in physical memory has been modified since it was last loaded from disk. The dirty bit helps the OS track which pages need to be written back to disk when they are evicted from physical memory, reducing unnecessary writes and improving performance.

6. How is memory address translation performed in Linux?

A: Memory address translation in Linux is performed by the Memory Management Unit (MMU) in the CPU. The MMU uses the page table of the currently executing process to translate virtual addresses generated by the process into physical addresses that correspond to actual locations in physical memory.

7. How is the Translation Lookaside Buffer (TLB) related to the page table?

A: The TLB is a hardware cache used by the MMU to speed up memory address translation. It stores recently used virtual-to-physical address mappings, reducing the need to access the page table in memory frequently. When a virtual address is requested, the MMU first checks the TLB, and if the translation is found, it is used directly, avoiding a more time-consuming access to the page table.

8. What is demand paging?

A: Demand paging is a memory management technique where pages of a process are loaded into memory only when they are actually needed. Instead of loading the entire process into memory at once, demand paging brings in only the pages that are required for the process's current execution. This approach reduces the initial memory footprint and improves memory utilization.

9. What is a page fault?

A: A page fault is an exception or interrupt that occurs when a process attempts to access a page of virtual memory that is not currently present in physical memory (RAM). When a page fault happens, the OS must handle it by loading the required page from disk into physical memory and updating the page table to reflect the new mapping.

10. What is memory swapping?

A: Memory swapping is the process of moving entire processes or parts of processes from RAM to disk (swap space) when physical memory becomes scarce. It helps free up RAM for other processes and allows the system to continue running even when the total memory demand exceeds the physical memory capacity.

11. What is a swap file?

A: A swap file is a dedicated file on a disk partition that serves as swap space in a virtual memory system. It is used to store pages of memory that are swapped out from RAM when memory resources are limited. The swap file provides an extension to the available virtual memory space beyond the physical RAM installed in the system.

Chapter 5:

1. What is the difference between brk() and sbrk() system calls?

A: The brk() system call sets the program break pointer to a specific address while the sbrk() system call increments the program break pointer by a given number of bytes.

2. How does the brk() system call modify the program break pointer of a process?

A: The brk() system call sets the program break pointer to a specific address. This address becomes the end of the data segment and the start of the heap.

3. What is the purpose of the sbrk() system call in memory allocation?

A: The sbrk() system call is used to increment the program break pointer to dynamically allocate memory on the heap.

4. Can the sbrk() system call allocate a continuous memory block of arbitrary size in a process' heap?

A: Yes, sbrk() system call can increment the program break pointer to allocate a continuous block of memory of any size on the heap.

5. How does the malloc() function utilize the sbrk() system call to allocate memory on the heap?

A: When malloc() function is called, it uses sbrk() system call to increment the program break pointer and allocate memory on the heap. malloc() then manages the allocated memory by creating a heap data structure to track the blocks of memory that have been allocated.

6. What happens when a program calls the malloc() function with a size greater than the available free memory on the heap?

A: If malloc() function is called with a size greater than the available free memory on the heap, it uses sbrk() system call to request more memory from the operating system.

7. How does the free() function release memory allocated by malloc() back to the heap?

A: When the free() function is called, it updates the heap data structure to mark the memory block as free and adds it to the free list for later reuse.

8. Can free() return memory to the OS when the released memory is at the end of the heap?

A: No, the free() function cannot return memory to the OS when the released memory is at the end of the heap. The OS cannot reclaim the memory until the program terminates.

9. What happens when a program calls free() with an invalid memory address?

A: When the free() function is called with an invalid memory address, it can result in a segmentation fault or undefined behavior. Therefore, it is important to ensure that the memory address passed to free() is valid and points to a block of memory that was previously allocated using malloc().

10. How does the free list help optimize memory allocation and deallocation in a program that uses malloc() and free() functions?

A: The free list is a linked list data structure that keeps track of the free memory blocks in the heap. When a program calls malloc(), the malloc() function first checks the free list to see if there is a block of memory that can be reused before requesting additional memory from the OS. This helps optimize memory allocation and can reduce the number of calls to sbrk(). Similarly, when the free() function is called, it adds the released memory block to the free list so that it can be reused in future calls to malloc().

Chapter 6:

1. What is a signal in the context of the Linux kernel?

A: A signal is a software interrupt delivered to a process by the OS kernel.

2. How are signals used to communicate with processes in Linux?

A: Signals are used to notify a process that an event has occurred, such as a user pressing Ctrl+C on the keyboard.

3. What is the difference between a synchronous and an asynchronous signal?

A: A synchronous signal is delivered immediately to a process while an asynchronous signal is queued and delivered at a later time.

4. How does a process handle a signal that is sent to it?

A: When a process receives a signal, it can either ignore the signal, perform a default action, or execute a signal handler that has been registered for that signal.

5. What are some common signals in Linux and what are their default actions?

A: Some common signals in Linux include SIGINT (Interrupt), SIGTERM (Termination), SIGHUP (Hangup), SIGKILL (Kill), and SIGUSR1/SIGUSR2 (User-defined signals). The default actions are specific to each signal, such as termination or ignoring the signal.

6. Can a process change the default action for a specific signal in Linux? If so, how?

A: Yes, a process can change the default action for a specific signal using the signal() or sigaction() system calls to register a custom signal handler.

7. What is the purpose of the kill command in Linux and how is it used to send signals to processes?

A: The kill command is used to send a signal to a process. Its primary purpose is to terminate a process, but it can also be used to send other signals to a process.

8. How does the nohup command interact with signals in Linux?

A: The nohup command is used to run a command with hangup signals ignored, ensuring that the process will not be terminated when the user logs out of the terminal.

9. What is the difference between the SIGINT and SIGTERM signals?

A: The SIGINT signal is sent to a process when the user presses Ctrl+C, typically asking the process to terminate gracefully. On the other hand, the SIGTERM signal is used to explicitly terminate a process.

10. Can a process ignore a signal that is sent to it in Linux? If so, how?

A: Yes, a process can ignore a signal that is sent to it by registering a signal handler that performs no action or ignores the signal.

Chapter 7:

1. What is the purpose of process scheduling in Linux?

A: The purpose of process scheduling in Linux is to allocate CPU time to running processes in an efficient and fair manner.

2. How does the Linux scheduler decide which process to run next?

A: The Linux scheduler uses a variety of algorithms and heuristics to decide which process to run next, taking into account factors such as process priorities, CPU usage, and I/O operations.

3. What are the different states a process can be in and how do they relate to scheduling?

A: A process can be in several different states, including running, sleeping, waiting, stopped, traced, and zombie.

4. Can a process receive signals in any state? If not, which states prevent a process from receiving signals?

A: A process can receive signals in any state, except for the stopped and traced states.

5. How does the nice command affect process scheduling in Linux?

A: The nice command allows you to adjust the priority of a process, which can affect its scheduling behavior.

6. What is the default niceness value for a process and how does it affect scheduling?

A: The default niceness value for a process is 0, and higher values correspond to lower priority.

7. How can you check the niceness value of a running process in Linux?

A: You can use the ps or top commands to check the niceness value of a running process in Linux.

8. How can you change the niceness value of a running process in Linux?

A: You can use the renice command to change the niceness value of a running process in Linux.

9. What is a signal in Linux and how is it used to communicate with a process?

A: In Linux, a signal is a software interrupt that can be sent to a process to request its attention or trigger a specific action.

10. How does a process handle signals in Linux?

A: A process can handle signals in Linux by registering a signal handler function to respond to specific signals.

11. What is the difference between a synchronous and asynchronous signal in Linux?

A: A synchronous signal is delivered immediately to a process during normal execution while an asynchronous signal can be delivered at any time, including during a system call or another operation.

12. Can a process ignore a signal in Linux? If so, how?

A: A process can ignore a signal by registering a null signal handler for that signal.

13. What is the difference between a signal handler and a signal mask in Linux?

A: A signal handler is a function that is called when a specific signal is received by a process while a signal mask is a set of signals that are currently blocked and will not be delivered to the process.

14. How does process scheduling in Linux relate to interrupt handling and timers?

A: Process scheduling in Linux is closely related to interrupt handling and timers, which are used to trigger context switches and schedule processes to run.

15. Can you explain how process scheduling works in Linux, including the role of the run queue and blocked queue?

A: The Linux scheduler uses run queues and blocked queues to manage the scheduling of processes, with processes being added to the appropriate queue based on their state and priority.

Chapter 8:

1. What is a file descriptor in Linux?

A: A file descriptor is a non-negative integer used to identify an open file or stream in a process.

2. How are file descriptors used in Linux?

A: File descriptors are used by processes to perform I/O operations on files, sockets, pipes, and other streams.

3. What is the maximum number of file descriptors a process can have in Linux?

A: The maximum number of file descriptors a process can have in Linux is typically determined by the value of the RLIMIT_NOFILE resource limit.

4. What is the open file table in Linux?

A: The open file table is a data structure maintained by the Linux kernel that keeps track of all the files and devices currently open in the system.

5. What information does the open file table contain?

A: The open file table contains information about each open file or device, such as the file's current offset, the file's mode (e.g., read-only, write-only, or read-write), and the file's access permissions.

6. How is the open file table different from a process's file descriptor table?

A: The open file table is a system-wide data structure that is shared by all processes in the system, whereas each process has its own file descriptor table that maintains information about the files and devices that the process has opened.

7. How does a process open a file in Linux?

A: A process can open a file in Linux by calling the open() system call, which returns a file descriptor the process can use to perform I/O operations on the file.

8. How does the kernel choose a file descriptor number for a newly opened file descriptor?

A: The kernel chooses the lowest available file descriptor number that is not already in use by the process.

9. What happens when a process reads from or writes to a file using a shared file descriptor?

A: When a process reads from or writes to a file using a shared file descriptor, the kernel updates the metadata in the corresponding entry in the open file table.

10. What happens when a process closes a file descriptor?

A: When a process closes a file descriptor, the kernel removes the corresponding entry from the process's file descriptor table and decrements the reference count for the corresponding entry in the open file table. If the reference count drops to zero, the kernel releases the resources associated with the file or device.

11. How can a process share a file descriptor with another process in Linux?

A: A process can share a file descriptor with another process by using the fork() system call to create a new process that inherits a copy of the parent process's file descriptor table.

12. Can multiple processes share the same file descriptor in Linux?

A: Yes, multiple processes can share the same file descriptor in Linux if they have inherited a copy of the same file descriptor table from a parent process.

13. What happens when two processes share a file descriptor in Linux?

A: When two processes share a file descriptor, they are both referring to the same entry in the open file table, which means that they can both perform I/O operations on the file or device.

14. How does the kernel handle concurrent access to a shared file descriptor?

A: The kernel uses locks to ensure that concurrent access to a shared file descriptor is synchronized and serialized so that each process sees a consistent view of the file or device's metadata.

15. How does the dup() system call work in Linux?

A: The dup() system call in Linux duplicates an existing file descriptor, creating a new file descriptor that refers to the same open file description. The allocated file descriptor number for the new descriptor is the lowest available non-negative integer that is not already in use by the process.

16. How does the dup2() system call work in Linux?

A: The dup2() system call in Linux is used to duplicate an existing file descriptor to a specific desired file descriptor number. If the desired file descriptor number is already in use, dup2() first closes that file descriptor before duplicating the source file descriptor. This ensures that the new file descriptor refers to the same open file description as the source, and it has the specified file descriptor number.

Chapter 9:

1. What is a file system?

A: A file system is a method or structure used by OSs to organize and store data on storage devices, such as hard drives and solid-state drives. It provides a hierarchical structure for organizing files, directories, and other information, enabling efficient storage, retrieval, and management of data on the storage device.

2. What is an inode table?

A: An inode table, also known as an inode array, is a data structure used in many file systems, including ext2, ext3, and ext4, to store metadata information about files and directories. Each entry in the inode table represents an inode, which contains attributes of a specific file or directory, such as permissions, owner, size, timestamps, and pointers to the data blocks that hold the file's content.

3. What is a direct pointer?

A: A direct pointer is a type of pointer used in a file's inode to directly reference data blocks storing the file's contents. In file systems like ext2, ext3, and ext4, the first twelve pointers in the inode are direct pointers. Each direct pointer points to a specific data block, allowing for fast and direct access to the file's initial data blocks.

4. What is an indirect pointer?

A: An indirect pointer is a pointer used in a file's inode to indirectly reference data blocks that store the file's content. Instead of directly pointing to the data blocks, the indirect pointer points to a data block that contains an array of pointers. Each entry in this array points to a data block, extending the number of blocks accessible by the file.

5. What is a doubly indirect pointer?

A: A doubly indirect pointer is a type of pointer used in a file's inode to enable additional levels of indirection for accessing data blocks. It points to a data block that contains an array of pointers, similar to indirect pointers. However, each entry in this array points to another data block, which, in turn, contains an array of pointers to the actual data blocks that store the file's content. This allows for further extension of the number of accessible data blocks.

6. What is a directory?

A: A directory is a special type of file used in a file system to store a list of file names and their corresponding inodes. Directories organize files into a hierarchical structure, allowing users and applications to navigate and access files based on their names and locations within the directory tree.

7. What is a file?

A: A file is a named collection of data or information stored on a storage device. Files can contain various types of data, such as text, images, audio, video, or executable code. They are organized within directories and can be accessed, modified, and deleted by users and applications.

8. What is a hard link?

A: A hard link is a file system link that associates multiple directory entries with the same inode. All hard links pointing to the same inode refer to the same underlying data, effectively representing different names or paths that can be used to access the same file content. Changes made to the content of one hard-linked file are reflected in all other hard-linked files.

9. What is a symbolic link?

A: A symbolic link, also known as a soft link, is a special type of file that contains a reference to another file or directory. Unlike hard links, symbolic links point to the path of the target file or directory rather than directly to its inode. If the target file or directory is moved or deleted, the symbolic link becomes invalid.

10. What is the difference between a hard link and a symbolic link?

A: The main difference between a hard link and a symbolic link lies in how they reference files. A hard link directly associates multiple directory entries with the same inode, so all hard-linked files refer to the same underlying data. On the other hand, a symbolic link points to the path of the target file or directory, providing a more flexible reference, but does not directly share the same inode or underlying data.

11. What is a block?

A: A block is the smallest unit of data that can be read or written to a storage device. In file systems, files are divided into blocks, and data is stored in them. File systems typically allocate and manage disk space in terms of blocks, allowing efficient storage and retrieval of data.

12. What is a superblock?

A: A superblock is a critical data structure in a file system that stores metadata about the file system itself. It contains information such as the total number of inodes and blocks, the size of each block, the location of the inode table, and other file system parameters. The superblock is usually located at a fixed position on the storage device and is crucial for mounting and accessing the file system.

13. What is a file descriptor?

A: A file descriptor is an integer value that serves as a reference to an open file within a process. It is used by OSs to track and manage open files on behalf of a process. File descriptors are typically used for input and output operations on files, sockets, and other I/O resources.

14. What is a file system driver?

A: A file system driver, also known as a file system module or file system handler, is software that enables an OS to interact with a specific file system format. Each file system type requires a dedicated file system driver to provide the necessary routines and functions for reading, writing, and managing files on the underlying storage device.

15. What is a file system mount point?

A: A file system mount point is a directory within an existing file system where another file system is attached and made accessible. When a file system is "mounted" at a mount point, the files and directories in the mounted file system become accessible from the mount point directory.

16. What is a file system journal?

A: A file system journal, also known as a journaling file system, is a technique used in some modern file systems to improve reliability and reduce data corruption in case of unexpected system crashes or power failures. The journal records changes before they are applied to the main file system structures, allowing faster recovery and reducing the chances of file system inconsistencies.

Chapter 10:

1. What is a socket?

A: A socket is a communication endpoint that allows processes to communicate with each other over a network.

2. What types of sockets are available in Linux?

A: Linux supports several types of sockets, including TCP/IP sockets, UDP sockets, raw sockets, and Unix domain sockets.

3. What is the difference between a TCP/IP socket and a UDP socket?

A: TCP/IP sockets provide reliable, connection-oriented communication between processes while UDP sockets provide unreliable, connectionless communication.

4. What is a Unix domain socket?

A: A Unix domain socket is a type of socket available in Unix-like OSs that provides a mechanism for Inter-Process Communication (IPC) between processes on the same machine.

5. How do you create a Unix domain socket?

A: To create a Unix domain socket in Linux, you can use the socket() system call with the AF_UNIX address family.

6. How do you bind a Unix domain socket to a file system path?

A: To bind a Unix domain socket to a file system path in Linux, you can use the bind() system call with a sockaddr_un structure containing the path.

7. How do you listen for incoming connections on a Unix domain socket?

A: To listen for incoming connections on a Unix domain socket in Linux, you can use the listen() system call.

8. How do you accept incoming connections on a Unix domain socket?

A: To accept incoming connections on a Unix domain socket in Linux, you can use the accept() system call.

9. How do you connect to a Unix domain socket from a client process?

A: To connect to a Unix domain socket from a client process in Linux, you can use the connect() system call with a sockaddr_un structure containing the path.

10. What programming languages provide native support for Unix domain sockets?

A: Many programming languages provide native support for Unix domain sockets, including C/C++, Python, Ruby, Java, Go, and Rust.

Chapter 11:

1. What is the role of the BIOS/UEFI in the boot process?

A: The BIOS/UEFI firmware initializes the hardware components and performs a Power-On Self-Test (POST) to check their functionality.

2. What is a boot loader?

A: A boot loader is a program that loads the OS kernel into memory and starts its execution.

3. What is the function of the Linux kernel during boot?

A: The Linux kernel is responsible for detecting and configuring the hardware devices, mounting the root file system, and starting the init process.

4. What is the root file system?

A: The root file system is the top-level directory hierarchy containing all the files and directories needed to run the OS.

5. What is an init system?

A: An init system is a program that starts and stops system services and daemons and runs scripts during the boot process.

6. What is the difference between systemd and SysVinit?

A: systemd is a modern init system that aims to improve system boot time and simplify service management while SysVinit is an older init system that uses shell scripts for service management.

7. What is a user session?

A: A user session is a period of time during which a user interacts with the system, typically through a graphical desktop environment or a command-line interface.

8. What happens if the kernel fails to boot?

A: If the kernel fails to boot, the system may display an error message or enter a kernel panic state, which requires a manual restart or recovery process.

9. Can the boot process be customized?

A: Yes, the boot process can be customized by modifying the configuration files of the boot loader, kernel, and init system and by adding or removing startup scripts and services.

10. What is the difference between a cold boot and a warm boot?

A: A cold boot, also known as a hard boot, is when the computer is turned on or restarted from a completely powered-off state A warm boot, also known as a soft boot or restart, is when the computer is restarted without powering it off completely. In a warm boot, some parts of the system, such as the contents of memory or some device configurations, may be preserved from the previous session.

www.ingramcontent.com/pod-product-compliance
Lightning Source LLC
LaVergne TN
LVHW072050060326
832903LV00054B/380